Manager

■ ■ ■

About the Author

Gareth Lewis B.Sc. (Hons), M.Sc. MIPD is a management consultant who works in the field of management and organisational
development. He has been involved in the design and delivery of a
wide range of programmes and projects.

He is a senior associate of the Institute of Management. Over many
years he has been involved in teaching and supporting people on
learning programmes of various kinds across all sectors of
industry, both in the UK and abroad. He was involved in the development of the Institute's Certificate and Diploma programmes, and
of the approach to mentoring within those programmes. As well as
actively mentoring learners, he has trained literally hundreds of
mentors.

He has written many books on management and presented papers
at a number of conferences on mentoring.

The Institute of Management (IM) is at the
forefront of management development and
best management practice. The Institute
embraces all levels of management from
students to chief executives. It provides a
unique portfolio of services for all managers,
enabling them to develop skills and achieve
management excellence.

If you would like to hear more about the
benefits of membership, please write to
Department P, Institute of Management,
Cottingham Road, Corby NN17 1TT.

This series is commissioned by the
Institute of Management Foundation.

The Mentoring Manager

Strategies for fostering talent and spreading knowledge

■ ■ ■

GARETH LEWIS

the Institute
of Management
FOUNDATION
PITMAN
PUBLISHING

London · Hong Kong · Johannesburg
Melbourne · Singapore · Washington DC

Many of the approaches in this book owe a great deal to the ideas of Steve Carter and Dr Brian O'Neill. My thanks go to them.

PITMAN PUBLISHING
128 Long Acre, London WC2E 9AN
Tel: +44 (0) 171 447 2000
Fax: +44 (0) 171 240 5771

A Division of Pearson Professional Limited

First published in Great Britain 1996

© Pearson Professional Limited 1996

The right of Gareth Lewis to be identified as author
of this work has been asserted by him in accordance
with the Copyright, Designs and Patents Act 1988.

ISBN 0 273 62344 3

British Library Cataloguing in Publication Data
A CIP catalogue record for this book can be obtained from the British Library.

10 9 8 7 6 5 4 3 2 1

Typeset by Northern Phototypesetting Co Ltd, Bolton
Printed and bound in Great Britain by Bell and Bain Ltd, Glasgow

The Publishers' policy is to use paper manufactured from sustainable forests.

Contents

■ ■ ■

Introduction		x
1 Why mentoring?		1
The natural history of mentoring		2
The changing world of work		3
How should managers cope?		5
The changing world of learning		7
Why mentoring?		9
Who gains from mentoring?		11
2 The mentoring wheel		19
Mentoring as a natural process		21
Mentoring at work		22
The organisation base		27
The context base		28
The development base		28
The interpersonal base		29
Role models		30
3 Who can mentor?		37
Skills, qualities, attributes		38
Who should choose mentors?		48
Should line managers be mentors?		51
Training mentors		52
4 The organisational perspective		57
Individual relationship versus corporate scheme		59
Internal versus external mentors		62
The influence of organisational culture		63
What is culture?		63
Why is culture important?		64
The role of interpreter		68
The role of advocate		69
The mentor as a role model		71

5 The uses of mentoring 77

The dimensions of mentoring relationships 82
The points of focus within the four-base model 84
Further applications 89
The role of process adviser or consultant 90

6 Helping people to learn 95

The role of the manager 97
Adults are sophisticated learners 98
Learner confidence 98
The Kolb learning cycle 100
Using the learning cycle 102
Learning styles 104
Using learning styles 106
Mentor–learner pairings 107
Role models 109
The 3-dimensional approach to coaching 111
Good managers are natural coaches 115
Other issues that affect learning activities 115

7 Mentoring relationships 119

The interpersonal frame 120
The nature of one-to-one relationships 123
Counselling 127
When to counsel 128
The 3-dimensional approach to counselling 129
Counselling style 132
Letting go 133

8 The mentoring manager 137

Phase I: Initiation 139
Phase II: Growth and performance 143
Phase III: Maturity 151

9 The learners' experience 155

What learners want 159
Fears and uncertainties 162
Preparing learners for mentoring 164
Change 165
What happens if things go wrong? 167

10 Mentoring programmes 173

Setting up a mentoring programme 177
What can go wrong? 185

11 Getting started 189

Me 191
Them 191
First session 193
Coaching vs counselling vs mentoring 195
Support 196
How do I ...? 196

The 'One Stop' Mentor 203

Index 209

'People who grew up in difficult circumstances and yet are successful have one thing in common; at a critical juncture in their adolescence, they had a positive relationship with a caring adult.'

Bill Clinton, President of the United States

Introduction

■ ■ ■

It isn't just children who need mentoring. We all do. Mentoring has been shown to be one of the most effective forms of intervention in terms of helping people to develop in their jobs and careers. Mentoring is unique in its place as a method of supporting people in learning and career development in that it does not exclude other methods, but exists alongside them, complementing them and adding value.

There are two basic circumstances that come together to make mentoring so important. One is the efficacy of mentoring, already mentioned. The other is the increasingly strong requirement for people to change as the world changes around them. That mentoring is seen as being central to many of these changes can be seen in the massive growth in interest in the subject. In 1980 there were about twelve references to articles on mentoring in the ABI/Inform database. By 1995 this number had grown to about eighty-five. These ideas are explored more fully in Chapter 1.

The role of the manager is critical in the growth in practice and importance of mentoring. It is the responsibility of managers to develop their staff, and managers are natural candidates as mentors. All managers should be seeking to add the skills of mentoring to their repertoire.

This book sets out the basic description of the concept: what it is, how it can be used, what skills are required. It also provides many ideas on how to go about it. Readers should be able to use the book to provide themselves with the conceptual framework and the tools to apply that framework to their own applications.

A topic like mentoring can be daunting when people first come across it, so I have organised the concepts of mentoring into a device called the 'mentoring wheel', which should help to translate the ideas into very practical action in real-life situations.

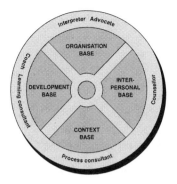

A wheel is an apt metaphor as it implies travel or movement. I hope you will find the book a useful companion on your journey.

'Managers need not only to develop themselves, but to take a much more active role in communicating with and developing their own team.'

Chapter 1

■ ■ ■

Why mentoring?

■ *Key learning points*

1 The world of business and the world of work are changing. These changes put new pressures and bring new imperatives for the manager

2 There has been a re-evaluation of the way that people learn at work, and these need new methods of delivery and support

3 Mentoring is seen as a valuable tool in these processes which has benefits for all concerned

Mentoring is one of those terms that seems to have become very fashionable in the 1990s. All of a sudden everyone seems to be talking about it and doing it. But where does this interest come from? Why has it become so important? The aim of this chapter is to give an explanation and a rationale for this phenomenon, and to explain why it really is important to understand and use mentoring.

The natural history of mentoring
■ ■ ■

The first thing that should be said, and most people realise this, is that mentoring is not new at all. Its roots go all the way back to Greek mythology (where the term comes from). If you read newspapers or biographies, you will soon see that in the worlds of literature and the arts, the sciences and sport, in fact in almost any field of human achievement, the top performers invariably cite someone they refer to as a mentor, as a source of inspiration.

Apart from ancient mythology, we can see that mentoring or mentoring-type relationships have evolved quite naturally in many contexts over history. The notion of apprenticeship, from the Middle Ages, has had connotations of older, wiser practitioners 'bringing along' or instructing younger, less experienced apprentices. This was how the artists of Renaissance Italy learned their trade. And so this process comes right up to date, in that the term is used in a huge and diverse variety of real-life contexts.

These so-called 'mentors' are usually older and wiser people, who have a wide knowledge and experience of the world in general, and the specific area of activity or knowledge in particular. They are often quoted as having substantial influence over budding performers during their formative years. It is interesting that the notion of learning, growing and developing is almost wired in to the concept as we understand and use it.

The other important implication of mentoring, of course, is that it is a perfectly natural process, and is a part of the way that we, as humans, pass on knowledge, skill and experience to others.

These 'real-life' or natural mentors needed no instruction on how to mentor. They have attended no courses (and probably haven't read books like this one!). We should be encouraged by this – that mentoring seems to be a natural skill that some people have, and that the role itself has developed organically in human relations.

That does not mean, of course, that we can't learn about the role. In fact, one of the great challenges for us is to learn how to apply the concept within the world of work, in a structured, thoughtful and planned way, by not only retaining, but also by enhancing the natural skill.

The changing world of work

■ ■ ■

As an explanation for the current prominence and necessity for mentoring, we need to look at the world of work. We need to examine what it is about that world that requires us to create and exploit new roles like mentoring.

3

The economy is changing

The economic environment is changing fast. In the UK we have seen a shift from manufacturing to a service-dominated economy. As we have moved through the 'boom and bust' eighties and into the nineties, we have seen a slow-down in growth that looks likely to remain.

Other seismic changes have occurred all over the world. We have seen the emergence of the growing manufacturing importance of the Pacific Rim, and the entry into the world economy of large populations like those of China.

The pace of development of technology and the coming of the Information Age have also had major influences. Organisations have to move fast to keep up.

The market is changing

It is said that consumers are becoming 'greyer, greener and

wiser'. The focus in the market place has moved from basic commodity products to more sophisticated added-value products and services. Organisations compete by differentiating not just by technological innovation, but by adding service and intangible elements to build brands. The pace of change in technology means that any technical lead is likely to be short-lived, before it is copied, and copied cheaper somewhere else.

Competition, then, is fierce, and customers are becoming ever more demanding. We are seeing not just a European perspective, but a global one, in terms of marketing and resourcing.

Organisations are changing

In order to meet these challenges, organisations are having to change radically and dramatically. Flatter and leaner have become almost a cliché. Organisations are having to invent new structures to meet the changing demands of the market place. These changes are also designed to enable organisations to adapt to change more fluidly and efficiently.

Often, line management has been replaced by semi-autonomous or self-managed work teams. All of these changes are designed to distribute power, authority and initiative throughout the organisation. There are fewer people at work, and those who remain have to work harder to produce, and also have to work harder to compete and to keep up.

Organisations that can adapt to the changes both in the external environment and in their internal structures and processes in a positive and planned way are called learning organisations.

The world of work is changing

Alongside the changes in organisational structures are changes in culture. One of the key words of the nineties is 'empowerment'. Responsibility for decision-making and action is being distributed throughout organisations at every level, rather than being invested in a chosen few, at the top of the tree.

Work practices are becoming less rule bound, and creativity and

4

innovation at the production end and at the customer interface are becoming key. For management, delayering means more work, more responsibility and more decisions.

Relationships are changing

The fact that organisations are growing, contracting and changing so fast has implications for people as employees. Most people are only too well aware that jobs for life are a thing of the past. Employment contracts are now beginning to reflect this. Salary and progression are only two aspects of current employment contracts. They are now as likely to encompass conditions, other benefits and entitlement to professional development. We are entering the era of the psychological contract. Employment is likely to deliver a range of benefits both ways, but increasingly it will be temporary, before the employee moves on to the next stage of his/her career.

Obviously, one of the major implications of these cumulative factors is that employment becomes more demanding and less stable. In order to keep abreast of the changes, it is necessary to keep moving and keep developing. It is this imperative that is the basis for much of the interest in mentoring.

5

How should managers cope?
■ ■ ■

The people who are caught between the strategic centre, the workforce and the customers in all of these changes are, of course, the managers. It is the management of an organisation that is having to deal with these dramatic changes. In order to do this, managers are having to develop a new set of skills and approaches to enable them to cope.

In *Management Development to the Millennium* the Cannon and Taylor Working Party Reports (An IM Research report, July 1994), it was reported that managers:

> continually referred to three key features that describe or impact upon the current and future business environment. These are:
>
> ■ The real sense of being 'battered' by the recession.
>
> ■ A future of rapid, violent and discontinuous change.

In many aspects of its operations, an individual organisation will be seeking to achieve simultaneously two or more contradictory goals.

In the same report the pressures on modern managers were described in relation to a number of paradoxes, which defined some of the contradictory pressures on managers. These included:

- Consolidation versus growth

- Future planning versus short-term pressures

- Long-term tasks versus instant solutions

- Internal focus versus external relations

- External pressures versus internal solutions

- International cooperation versus economic nationalism

- Informed markets versus militant consumerism.

If these are some of the pressures on working managers, then clearly managers will have to change and adapt in order to maintain success. So what does this mean for individual managers? Some of the priorities for their own development include:

- New styles of management

- Increased delegation of responsibility

- Multi-skilling

- New forms of communication supported by technology

- Continuous learning.

Their role will increasingly become one of 'developing the organisational structure and the people within it so that it can self-generate'. What this means in practice is that managers will increasingly have to become facilitators, empowerers and developers of other people.

- **Empowerment.** With fewer managers and more responsibility, each manager will have to delegate more to members of the team. The role shifts from controller to that of goal-setter and monitor. This, in turn, leads to much more emphasis on the 'softer' skills. Negotiating and influencing are becoming more important than directing and controlling.

- **Developing.** As the world changes, so we and our staff must change with it. Those people reporting directly to managers must themselves take on more responsibility. In order to do this they need to develop and learn. The most effective and successful managers will be those who can recruit, develop and motivate the best teams. Fostering learning and development in the workplace is already a key skill.

- **Facilitating and managing change.** The move away from the polarity of either performing tasks or controlling and directing the work of others implies a new kind of 'three-dimensional' role. This is that of the facilitator. A facilitator is one who enables and supports the work of others.

This new set of skills implies a very new kind of role for the manager. This role itself involves developing and adapting for managers themselves, but it also involves taking a leading part in the development of other staff. A shift to the softer, more people-centred skills, and a focus on learning and development are the key features of this new role.

7

There are some key themes that come out of all of this. One is that learning is going to be the key for all managers. The learning is going to be continuous and never-ending. What we now know tells us that we can't be trained with a particular set of skills and hope that these will last for a life-time, or even for a number of years. Another change that goes alongside this, and is implicit in all that has been said, is that the manager will have to take responsibility for his/her own learning.

The changing world of learning
■ ■ ■

Not surprisingly, we are also changing in our attitudes and our approaches to learning. Take the world of management as an example. Traditionally, there were very few systematic ways to learn how to be a manager. In most areas of business (including the maintained and non-profit making sectors), people were promoted on the basis of their technical or functional skills. From here they were supposed to somehow be magically transformed into managers. Of course, it doesn't work quite like that. In the worst cases people do not make a success of the management role because the set of skills required for managing is perhaps different from those they were previously good at. Many a good teacher has turned out to be a poor headteacher. Of course, many people survive by the age-old development process – getting it wrong first time round, but gradually learning by experience and by their own mistakes.

When people did start to look at the systematic development of managers, the results were either short, *ad hoc* training courses or knowledge and exam-based certificated courses. There are a number of potential problems with the latter approach. First, it is quite difficult to get significant transfer of learning to work. Secondly, given the business environment painted above, it is becoming increasingly difficult to take people out of work for extended courses off-the-job. Finally, we are just developing much richer and more sophisticated ideas about how adults can learn at work. This is reflected in the more varied means of achieving learning.

8

If we look at the proposed methods by which people intend to develop themselves we see the following list:

- External courses
- Job rotation
- On-the-job training
- Internal courses
- Project work
- Self-managed learning
- Workplace experience and practice
- Action learning
- Role modelling
- Peer-group contacts
- Private reading
- Work shadowing

- Coaching and tutoring

- Delegated tasks

- Learning contracts

- Distance learning

- Programmed learning

- Secondment

- Job enrichment

- Community activities

- Internal conferences/seminars

- Projects

- Study visits

- Job shadowing.

9

Mentoring can itself be considered one of the list – as a way of delivering direct learning. However, it also plays an interesting role in that it can also be an 'overarching process' that can sit above, complement or support the others.

This repertoire of methods is much more broadly focused, much less academically inclined and much more flexible than the training regimes of previous generations. Much more of this learning is clearly not only going to be managed by the individual, but is also increasingly going to take place at work.

Why mentoring?
■ ■ ■

The world of work is changing, and approaches to learning are changing, but we need to ask the question why is mentoring becoming so central to the delivery of learning at work? We know that people from a multitude of sources and experiences do believe that mentoring is important.

David Clutterbuck asked a group of 250 human resources specialists at the 1995 Institute of Personnel Development national conference at Harrogate: 'Who do you feel it easiest to learn from?' Mentoring came third in the list after peers and line managers.

He also asked: 'Who has the most potential for you to learn from?' Mentors came top, being selected by about half of the respondents.

This is interesting for a number of reasons. This shows clearly the potential that mentoring is perceived to have among those most responsible for developing people in organisations. However, it also shows that mentoring is not yet considered the easiest way to learn, and that may be due to the fact that many managers have yet to think about or develop fully their skills and capabilities in mentoring.

But what is it about mentoring that makes people think it has such a powerful potential in helping people to learn? It has a number of characteristics that can help to explain this.

- **It has flexibility.** Mentoring can happen in so many ways and in a wide variety of circumstances. There is no prescribed minimum set of rules or requirements for it to happen. The only necessities are time and at least two people.

- **It is an off-line activity.** It takes place out of the run of normal operational activity. Thus it has an element of informality and is more like a social than a purely professional or work-based activity.

- **It does relate to work and the job.** Although the style is not prescribed by work conventions, the substance can be highly work focused, and is therefore seen as practical.

- **It is individual.** It relates directly and uniquely to the needs and interests of the individual, in a way that few group development activities or remote development activities can.

- **It is people-centred.** It engages people as people, with all of their values, motives and feelings. It engages hearts as well as minds. Again, many other methods of delivering learning can't match this.

- **It is a feedback system.** Feedback is a structural component of a mentoring relationship. It is known to engage interest and attention, and also to enhance learning.

- **It is broad in focus.** Many of the other methods of learning, by their very nature, are located in specific personal, technical or functional skill areas. Mentoring, on the other hand, can encompass the whole range of working and human activity.

- **It is not exclusive.** One of the great advantages of mentoring is that it can be a coordinating, stimulating and monitoring process that operates in parallel or in addition to any or all of the other learning methods. If we choose mentoring, we don't have to 'unchoose' any of the others. In this sense, it is an 'added-value' activity.

Who gains from mentoring?

■ ■ ■

11

The answer is, of course, that everyone gains. Mentoring is an additive model. This should be of some reassurance to mentors or potential mentors. It is quite difficult to do any damage and it is easy to add something to the relationship for the individual involved.

Mentoring would be much less attractive and widespread if it were simply a one-dimensional activity from the mentor to the learner. All of the research and information that we have demonstrates quite strongly that all concerned gain from the relationship. However, it is worth looking at specific interest groups to examine what it is that mentoring can offer them. Let us look at the potential pay-offs.

Benefits for the learner

We have already mentioned that for most staff in organisations, particularly as they gain responsibility and seniority, they will need to take more responsibility for their own learning and development. Whether in a formal scheme or just an informal relationship, they will and should increasingly be seeking sources of guidance and support.

The major thrust of the benefit for the learner is that he/she gets support throughout the learning process. Specific benefits might depend on the context of the mentoring relationship. For instance, if the learner is in a systematic and structured learning programme, then a major benefit ought to be the successful completion of the course or accreditation. If the programme is about careers, counselling and advice, then the specific outcome should be easy to define.

However, the generic benefits that are likely to accrue for any learner include the following:

- **Greater understanding of the total organisational perspective.** Learners should be able to gain knowledge of an organisation outside of their own functional or business area. They may well pick up knowledge and understanding of how businesses work in general. They may also gain access to information, resources or other support structures from within the organisation, if the mentor is more senior. Finally, mentoring should help them to 'read' and understand the culture within the organisation.

- **Personal benefits.** As human beings, we have needs to socialise and affiliate with other people. We derive satisfaction from relationships, and a good mentor–learner relationship is no different from any other good relationship in that respect. The relationship might also work positively on our confidence and self-respect – particularly as we increase our skill and capability.

- **Learning outcomes.** These are at the core of the relationship. The development of skill and competence is one of the major benefits for the learner.

- **Developing his/her own learning to learn skills.** As we learn, so we become more confident and competent as learners. We will increasingly be able to focus explicitly on our own learning processes, approaches and styles.

- **Career benefits.** These may be an explicit part or purpose of the particular relationship. Whether it be induction, orientation or career advancement, the learner benefits from the intervention of the mentor.

- **Problem-solving and problem-solving approaches.** Learners are likely to use the medium of the relationship to help solve particular problems. This, in turn, will equip them more fully to tackle problems on their own.

- **Strengths and weaknesses.** There should be some analysis and some feedback on the strengths and weaknesses of the individual learner. This auditing process – and the analysis of development and learning needs – is part of a continuous and ongoing process.

Benefits for the mentor

The messages from the Cannon and Taylor Working Party are clear. Managers need not only to develop themselves, but also to take a much more active role in communicating with and developing their own team. In short, they need to empower their subordinates. They will thus become facilitators and supporters of learning. In other words, they will need to develop their mentoring role and the associated skills. The mentoring role of line managers will have a much greater significance and priority.

13

In many organisational contexts, people will be invited or required to play a role across functions for people over whom they will have no direct line-management responsibility. The value of the cross-functional or off-line mentor role will become increasingly important and is already growing fast. Many senior and experienced staff accept this responsibility not out of duty, but out of the satisfaction that the role can bring. In other words, they see it as enhancing their own role, skills and contributions.

The benefits here, again, depend on the particular context of the mentoring relationship. Also, if the mentor is a line manager for the learner, there ought to be specific pay-offs in terms of performance, efficiency or productivity.

However, there are also generic benefits and these include:

- **Business functions.** These can assist in scanning and monitoring performance within the organisation. They can also widen the scope and perspective for the mentor if the learner is from a different organisation, function or business unit.

- **Increases in personal satisfaction.** As with the learner, and for many of the same reasons, the mentor can get immense satisfaction from the relationship. In addition, the mentor can often feel that he/she is making a significant contribution to the system:

I wanted to get involved in helping with the kids' football, in the first place because of my own kids. But when they gave up I just carried on. As well as a bit of enjoyment and something useful to do for me, I felt I was giving something back because I had got such a lot from football as a kid. It wasn't the winning, or even just the matches, to be honest, that gave me the most pleasure. It was seeing those lads come on in leaps and bounds from the stage where they could hardly kick a ball.

- **Role enhancement and the expansion of repertoire of skills.** Mentors also have plenty to learn from the mentoring relationship. In the first instance, they are likely to learn about the role and skills associated with the mentoring itself. But they can also learn from their learners, if they are open enough to experience. The learners may have different functional or technical skills, some of which may rub off on to the mentors. The learners may have different approaches or styles, and may be strong where the mentors are weak.

- **Personal self-development.** The discipline and learning focus of the relationship is likely to be as much value to the mentor as the learner.

- **Career enhancement.** The career of the mentor can be enhanced in a number of ways. Clearly, this could be by virtue of the enhanced skill and role set. There are people who are proud (and shrewd enough) to describe their mentoring experience and skills in their CVs. Finally, mentoring can increase a manager's profile or visibility within an organisation. Along with profile, credibility and personal reputation can also increase.

Benefits for the organisation

Again, this depends to some extent on whether the mentoring is a systematic approach within the organisation to deliver specific outcomes. If it is, then the delivery of those outcomes will be its own benefit. Either way, there are some accrued and accumulated benefits within organisations where there are people receiving mentoring support. These include:

- **Better trained staff.** Mentoring is about learning, and effective learning involves improved performance at work. This not only improves skills, it may also improve morale.

- **Development of an organisational culture.** Mentoring, particularly if part of an organisation-wide scheme, initiates new channels of communication up, down and across an organisation. It develops new, more productive, supportive and 'people-centred' relationships.

- **More effective management development.** Remember, it is not just the learners who are being developed, but also the mentors. An organisation might train Mrs Jones as a mentor to someone from another department, but she may well be a different and better manager to her own staff as a result.

- **A positive orientation to learning.** Giving people not only new skills, but also an enhanced learning ability to develop new skills is a powerful blue touch paper to light. This is an important step in the direction of becoming a learning organisation.

- **Empowered staff.** Setting people on the track to learning increases their capability and increases their ability and their willingness to take responsibility.

15

■ *Mentoring action points*

This chapter should have provided you with plenty of good reasons to consider mentoring seriously – whether as a mentor or as a learner. To find out more for yourself and prepare for your role, you might consider the following:

- Talk to people who have been mentors and learners and find out about their experiences

- Think about what the role means to you and what you would like to gain from it

- Think about the next step.

'Mentoring is a relationship and a set of processes where one person offers help, guidance, advice and support to facilitate the learning or development of another person.'

Chapter 2

■ ■ ■

The mentoring wheel

■ *Key learning points*

1 By looking at natural mentoring relationships we can identify some important components of the mentor's role.

2 There are four basic reference points in any mentoring relationship. These are the four bases.

3 The mentoring wheel builds on these to include role descriptions, and these, in turn, are associated with a set of skills.

The purpose of this chapter is to examine the role of the mentor. We need to define an approach to mentoring that captures, in a simple but rich form, the diversity and complexity of the many versions of mentoring relationships that are to be found in many areas of human activity. There is a huge diversity. Take the following examples:

> 'Four classic breeds will be on show at the Royal Horse Gala at the National Exhibition Centre in Birmingham next week. ... The Lusitanos are under the direction of Luis Valenca Rodrigues, co-founder of the Portuguese Royal Riding School, whose mentor was the legendary Nuno Oliviera, one of the century's most influential dressage teachers.'

> 'I need to make an appointment to see my mentor next week, to review my progress on the costing project.'

We shall be looking in much more detail at the range and types of mentoring application in Chapter 5. However, a look at almost any newspaper interview with a 'star', or a read of any biography will reveal a description of, or reference to, someone called a mentor, or a mentor-type figure.

The variety of contexts in which such mentoring-type relationships are mentioned is also diverse. They cover almost every area of human activity and almost every period of history.

One of the difficulties in arriving at a definition or a single description of the business of mentoring is the sheer variety and complexity of mentoring relationships which occur. However, if we want to define mentoring, especially in a modern working context, we should be willing to learn from good past experience. A good place to look for guidance is to those relationships that we now recognise as mentor–protégé relationships, which have occurred quite naturally throughout history.

Mentoring as a natural process
■ ■ ■

There seem to be some strongly based natural human functions that have existed across periods of history and across cultures. These functions must have fairly deep roots in our inherited behaviour. And as such behaviours are so prevalent, they must have some sociological benefit or survival pay-off. The mentor–protégé relationship is one of those functions.

It seems to be that as people mature, they develop a desire or need to pass on skills and wisdom to the next generation. Of course, there are benefits for both.

The protégé shows a willingness to listen and learn, and gets the benefit of the attention and the acquired wisdom. The mentor gets the satisfaction of seeing someone learn from their hard-won experience and wisdom. Presumably, they also gain satisfaction from the respect thus paid to them. The instinct of the mentor is often of a paternal/maternal nature, but it operates not only with parents. Mentors are chosen for their wisdom or accumulated experience, their skill or their achievements.

21

Once we have achieved status for ourselves, and are perhaps past the peak of our own personal, physical or performance capability, then we seem to acquire a need to develop such performance in others. However, in these 'natural' mentoring contexts there do seem to be certain characteristics that even the most disparate versions of mentoring have in common. Here are some of them.

A deep personal relationship

These natural mentoring relationships seem to involve a high level of trust and mutual admiration. The learner trusts the mentor because of a combination of admiration and respect. This often comes about because of the way they are, or because of some past or current achievement of the mentor. The mentor respects the learner perhaps for his/her potential, talent or effort. There also seems to be a need to protect, nurture, look after and develop.

A focus on an area of skill, achievement or performance

If you look at the nature of these 'natural' mentoring relation-ships, they are very often focused on a particular area of human activity that represents a shared interest or need for the mentor and the protégé. Thus, we can see mentoring relationships from every discipline and field of activity, from music and the arts to sports or technical and academic disciplines like mathematics or science.

A focus on learning

It seems to be an implicit and accepted part of these relationships that they involve the learner developing, learning and improving in some area of human activity. In fact, that seems to be one of the major reasons for the existence of mentoring relationships.

22

Other characteristics that may seem obvious but should also be borne in mind are that the relationships usually develop volun-tarily and do not operate to a planned schedule or timetable. Of course, there are exceptions to these points and, in a sense, that just emphasises the difficulty of trying to characterise all men-toring relationships with a single, simple list of characteristics.

This is why, when you talk to anybody about mentoring, it is quite possible that they will be talking about something quite different from you. Most people seem to have a commonsense understanding of what mentoring is, but it is much more difficult to pin it down to a single description.

Mentoring at work
■ ■ ■

Considerations about natural mentoring are instructive and important. Obviously, it is important to keep the best of what works naturally. However, there are some important considera-tions and circumstances that must be taken into account when we are thinking about the notion of learning at work. One ques-tion is: is mentoring at work any different from the 'natural' model we have set out here?

The answer is, as you may expect, yes and no! It is the same in the sense that a natural inclination to certain kinds of nurturing or supporting relationships is an important strength to build on. The answer is no in that there are considerations and circumstances that operate in the working environment and in more structured and constructed relationships that don't necessarily operate in the more natural ones.

In order to apply the concept of mentoring to a working context, we need to give a definition of what we think mentoring is. There are many definitions available, all of which have some truth in the kinds of relationship we are looking at. It is quite difficult to find a definition which describes all of the different kinds of mentoring relationship that exist. In terms of mentoring at work, the most useful definition of mentoring is:

> *A relationship and a set of processes where one person offers help, guidance, advice and support to facilitate the learning or development of another person.*

23

In order to examine how mentoring in a working environment may be different from the natural model, we should look at a case study in some depth.

■ CASE STUDY

The Institute of Management 'Competent Manager Programme'

Vocational learning programmes began to shift the emphasis of their delivery and assessment from a traditional knowledge based approach to competence or performance based criteria, with the coming of the NVQ system. This process was also initiated in management training with the introduction of the Occupational Standards for Management in 1990. The IM Certificate programme was a modular programme which was delivered predominantly on an in-company basis. It involved a combination of self-study workbooks, workshops and individualised follow-up activity.

The self-study material was designed to provide the underpinning knowledge required to develop competence in a particular functional area. The workshops provided developmental experi-

▶

ences in relation to the required competences and focused on the application of knowledge and understanding to the learners' workplace activities.

Like many of the newer NVQ programmes, the programme presents learners with particular challenges. Some of these include:

- Learners need the opportunity to develop competence, often in a workplace environment, and will need the commitment and support of their organisation

- Learners need to learn skills of evidence collection and portfolio building

- Their route through the learning programme is individual and based on their own needs

- Learners are given responsibility for their own learning

- Many managers are returning to 'formal' learning for the first time in many years, and this brings problems, fears, apprehensions, and challenges learners' confidence

- Learners have to balance the learning programme with the demands of work.

It was decided that one of the major means of support for learners on the programme was that an individual mentor would be provided for each learner. Using an action research model and techniques such as repertory grid analysis, mentors and learners on a pilot programme were used to develop the role description of the mentor.

That role description and the programme have developed considerably in the years since 1990. However, there were some interesting results that emerged about the mentoring role right from the beginning.

The results

Seven key elements of competence emerged:

1 identifies and reviews the objectives, culture and needs of the learners' organisation to facilitate learning opportunities

2 communicates objectives and requirements of the programme to those members of the learners' organisation who will be involved

24

3 establishes the required level of support within the learners' organisation

4 provides constructive, assertive feedback to the learners

5 negotiates, oversees and reviews appropriate learning opportunities

6 maintains appropriate records and documents

7 creates and maintains clear agreement on the practical framework of the mentor–learner relationship

As well as this information, there was also a good deal of qualitative information that emerged from this process. As Steve Carter, Head of Management Development at the IM, said at the time:

> 'The quality of these interactions was remarked upon. These mentors had been good listeners, listening attentively and asking the sort of questions that helped the speaker clarify his/her own thoughts. They avoided authoritarian language, treated people as equal and encouraged people to think and act for themselves. They tolerated failure if the reasons for the failure were good. In addition, these mentors were not just good role models in their interpersonal skills, but in terms of their personal effectiveness in time management, personal organisation and professional competence. They could cope with ambiguity and were confident enough in their own position to relinquish control where appropriate, ensuring visible and practical support. In short, in the jargon of today, they empowered people.'

NVQs, and particularly NVQs in management, are a good example of the growth of mentoring. The mentors are there to support learners in a structured learning programme. This can be quite a tough challenge for the learners, as they have to cope not only with the development part of the programme, and with relating the learning to work, but also with the novel requirements of the NVQ process for the production of a portfolio of evidence for assessment of competence. This also places some challenging requirements on the mentor. Consider the following story.

'Last year I was approached by two of my team to act as mentor while they pursued a level 4 NVQ in management. My first reaction was panic and then pride that they had chosen to ask me. ▶

25

The next step was to find out what my involvement would be. A meeting was arranged with the college staff who were acting as assessors. They suggested that my role should be to guide and support [them] through the process.'

While a large part of mentoring involves confirming the validity of the evidence produced, a significant and very important aspect is to ensure that opportunities are given to candidates to allow them to undertake tasks to fill gaps in their knowledge/skills. Examples include:

■ Recruitment of staff

■ Presentation skills via an NVQ presentation

■ Organising a meeting and producing the minutes.

26

This case study suggests that mentoring can be about more than just the relationship between the mentor and the learner. In this case, the influence of the organisation and the requirements of the programme emerge very strongly as considerations.

The same message also featured strongly in the Competent Manager Programme. Much of what emerged concentrated, not surprisingly, on the nature and the quality of the individual relationship. What was different here, though, was that there appeared to be a number of items in the role description that were not often given too much thought or coverage. These were the items that focused on the organisation – its culture and the role or standing of the individual within it.

This suggested that for mentoring in a working environment to be successful, there was another area of consideration that needed to be added to the components of the traditional or natural model.

These ideas are illustrated in the four-base model of the mentoring process (Figure 1). These four bases provide the anchors or reference points for any mentoring relationship at work.

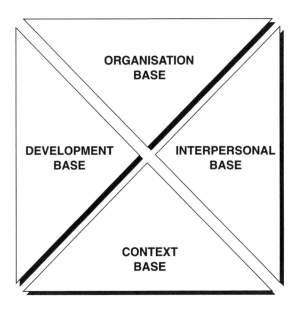

Fig 1   The four-base model of the mentoring process

What the model provides, then, is a framework within which we can describe the nature of the relationship and its important component parts. This model also has a more significant and more dynamic purpose. It can be used as a touchpoint or reference point for us to check that we understand and are quite explicit about what is entailed in this relationship. It also helps to define the rationale and the framework into which clusters of competences sit.

The organisation base
■ ■ ■

This has two basic areas of consideration. The first is the organisation itself, and the second relates to the expertise and experience of the individual mentors. There is also an interplay between the two components.

The organisation (or functional) base is about the position and experience of the mentor within the organisation. It is also about how the culture of the organisation impacts directly on the mentor–learner relationship.

If the mentor is to gain broad commitment to the objectives of the relationship and create or enable opportunities for the learner, then standing and access within the organisation are vital.

There are five basic questions:

- How will the culture of the organisation support the mentor–learner relationship?

- Is the culture enabling or inhibiting?

- Does the mentor have an understanding and perspective of the organisation?

- Does the mentor have credibility and influence within the organisation?

- Does the mentor have a high level of functional or technical expertise?

28

The context base
■ ■ ■

With mentoring in a working context there is usually a defined set of purposes that bind any particular relationship. In fact, a good deal of mentoring in any working context happens in quite structured learning or development programmes. These purposes or objectives, and the programmes in which they operate, provide an important foundation and rationale for the mentoring relationship. This is the context base. Clearly, mentors have a need to know the limits and scope of their role in relation to these particular requirements.

The development base
■ ■ ■

Whether it be the general development of people or supporting someone through a specific learning programme, learning and development are often at the centre of the mentor–learner relationship. Quite often it may indeed be the primary purpose of the relationship. If it is not, it is usually an important implicit or explicit secondary or complementary consideration.

The conditions and requirements of adults when they are learning at work need separate analysis. Mentors need to know something about how adults learn at work, and how they can act in ways that facilitate such learning. At a minimum, mentors need a developmental orientation and some personal experience of developmental situations.

The interpersonal base
■　■　■

This base points to the nature and quality of the one-to-one relationship between the mentor and the learner. It involves consideration of the values, strengths and motives of each of the individuals involved. It is also underwritten by the skills and attributes that are associated with communication.

The four-base approach is a good starting point in defining the important components of any mentoring relationship, especially when that relationship takes place in an organisational setting and has some agreed set of conditions, requirements or objectives that surround it. It can be used in a number of ways.

First, it can be used for those planning major initiatives involving a mentoring or support component. Whether this is a fairly loose set of arrangements or a formal programme, it is useful to use the approach as a benchmark set of considerations when planning and implementing.

Secondly, it can be used by individual mentors as a checklist to see if they have prepared themselves fully for the role. Have they covered all of the necessary considerations?

Finally, it can be used by human resources departments to plan, develop or design mentor training or briefing sessions.

However, in order for this to become a complete description of the mentoring concept and process, it needs enhancing with a number of other elements to encompass all of those other facets of human relationship behaviour.

The approach is simple yet rich enough that it acts as a natural integrating set of principles which brings all of these facets together in a simple model, called the *mentoring wheel*. The wheel is a good metaphor because it needs the hub, the spokes and the rim to keep it rigid. But, having all of the components, it can then get rolling.

In order for the four-base approach to have a high validity and utility for the practising mentor, it needs to incorporate all of these facets that are attached to the concept.

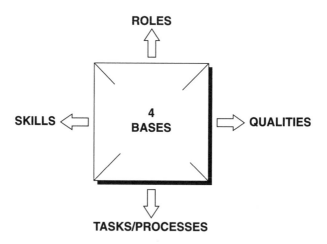

Fig 2   Aspects of the four bases

Let us take each of these facets of the role in turn.

Role models

■　■　■

The role models drop quite naturally out of the four-base considerations. It is worth pointing out that a complex and diverse role like mentoring cannot be described as a single role description. Each of the bases has a role, or set of roles, attached to it.

The *organisation base* is associated with the roles of:

- **Advocate or opportunity provider.** This is someone who can create opportunities for people to learn or to develop competence. The role is associated with the positional strength or the credibility within the organisation.

- **Interpreter.** Here, the mentor offers managerial or organisational perspectives based on their wider knowledge of this or other organisations. They are also transmitters of the culture of the organisation by virtue of knowing the ropes.

The *context base* is associated with the role of:

- **Process consultant.** In this role the mentor helps the learner to make sense of the broader requirements of the specific relationship (particularly if it is in a specific or structured learning programme). The mentor will be involved here with defining objectives, monitoring progress, solving problems, and so on.

The *development base* is associated with the roles of:

- **Learning consultant.** This is someone who is able to act as a consultant adviser or resourcer on matters associated with learning.

- **Coach.** Mentors quite often, by virtue of their wider and more senior experience or expertise, are able to coach their learners. That is, they can intervene directly to pass on knowledge and understanding, or to help them to develop skills.

The *interpersonal base* is associated with the role of:

- **Counsellor.** A counsellor is someone who acts in the best interest of an individual. They have a high degree of empathy and communication skills. Here, we don't mean a counsellor necessarily in the therapeutic sense of the term. We use it in a much broader sense to include friend, adviser, guide, guardian, and so on.

Each of these roles can be described in terms of a particular set of *skills* and is related to the personal *qualities* that any mentor might bring to the role.

All of these roles and requirements come together in a set of *tasks and processes* that define the progress of the mentor–learner nship. This whole array of interdependent factors is shown grated into the mentoring wheel (Figure 3).

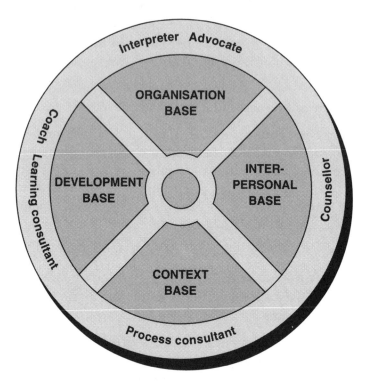

Fig 3   The mentoring wheel

In addition, we should set out some principles and assumptions about certain aspects of the nature of the relationship. Each relationship is different, and to a great extent this will be negotiated and agreed between the mentor and the learner at the outset of the relationship. We will discuss the detail of these terms of reference in Chapter 10. In the meantime, there are certain basic statements that need to be adhered to in any relationship.

- **Learners' responsibility.** Learners should be responsible, as self-directed adults for their own learning. This should include the responsibility for setting their own goals and making their own decisions.

- **Mentors' responsibility.** Mentors should envisage the relationship as helping the learners to help themselves.

- **Empowerment.** An important aim of the relationship is to enable the learners to feel and behave in an assertive and capable manner.

- **Judgement.** This should only be offered if it is invited. It is better that mentors base discussion on behaviour and performance rather than motives, personality or identity.

This model encapsulates all of the roles and processes of mentoring and provides us with a generic description of the process in its many and varied forms. It also enables us to answer questions that have previously been more difficult to pin down. Among these, there are two questions that people often ask:

- How is mentoring different from counselling?
- How is mentoring different from coaching?

The answer to the first question is that counselling is a feature or component of mentoring. We have already described it as but one of the mentoring roles. In that sense, then, mentoring is not different, but more, in that:

- it focuses on the organisation as well as the individual
- it happens in a context with aims, purposes, and so on
- it is about possibilities and capabilities as well as problems and difficulties
- it focuses on learning and development.

The answer to the second question is again that it is not so much different as more than just coaching. Coaching is one of the key roles within mentoring but it adds:

- a focus on learning and capability as well as skill
- a focus on the individual as well as the performance
- a broader context of aims and purposes.

33

■ *Mentoring action points*

We have now built a picture and set out a model of the total mentoring role. What is needed by a mentor or potential mentor is understanding and to be able to relate the mentoring wheel to his/her own experience.

- Could you describe the components of the mentoring wheel and the reasons why the four bases are important to someone else?

- Check with mentors and learners that you know if their experience corresponds to the four-base description. Which components were the easiest or the most difficult to deal with?

- Identify where you think your own strengths or weaknesses are in relation to the mentoring wheel.

In the following chapters we shall look at each of these areas in turn. We shall use the mentoring wheel to set out the role descriptions in some detail, and then we will move on to look at how mentors go about the various tasks and processes involved.

'Mentoring does not just happen: mentors and learners need to develop specific skills for their interactions to be effective.'

Chapter 3

■ ■ ■

Who can mentor?

■ *Key learning points*

1 There is a set of qualities that are strongly associated with good mentors.

2 These qualities can be used, together with an analysis of the four bases, to define the requirements for any context.

3 Mentors should be selected carefully and trained appropriately.

In this chapter we look at the skills, qualities and attributes that go to make a good mentor. We will look at some of the practical implications for selecting mentors for particular programmes and applications, and we will discuss how to go about training and briefing mentors to prepare them for the role.

One of the key questions that needs to be addressed is: who can mentor? Both organisations and prospective individual mentors will want to know what are the requirements of the job, and if they have the required skills and attributes.

Skills, qualities, attributes
■　■　■

If you look at any of the huge amount of articles and written material about mentoring that has appeared over the last few years, you can list the skills, qualities and attributes mentioned to try to build an identikit picture of what a good mentor should be. Here is a composite list of words that have been used to describe roles a mentor might take :

- guide ■ sponsor ■ counsellor ■ expert ■ source of knowledge ■ facilitator ■ coach ■ catalyst ■ role model ■ stimulator ■ energiser ■ friend ■ time-manager ■ diagnostician ■ goal-setter ■ taskmaster ■ planner ■ problem-solver ■ teacher ■ midwife.

Even this list is by no means exhaustive! The list of skills and qualities that can be attached to this list is even more extensive. You might like to try to list just a few key skills for each of the roles above. We clearly need some means of tidying up or organising this list to keep it to manageable proportions.

Research in the early 1990s identified a number of attributes or qualities in mentors that were highly valued by learners. A similar list was identified by mentors as being highly desirable qualities for the job. They were grouped into the following categories:

1. **Management perspective.** Someone who has experience of, and competence in, management. Alternatively, through experience working with managers in organisations, someone who has had widespread exposure to and understands management practice and pressures.

2. **Organisational know-how.** Someone who knows how to get things done within the organisational system in which the learner works.

3. **Credibility.** Someone who enjoys personal and professional credibility, either in his/her own right or with the members of the organisation in which the learner works.

4. **Accessibility.** Someone who is able to make him/herself available to others when they need it.

5. **Communication.** Someone who has a strong range of interpersonal skills and can tune in to others' ideas, views and feelings.

6. **Empowering orientation.** Someone who creates a climate and the conditions in which it is safe for individuals to try out different ways of doing things, to contribute more fully, and to have a greater share in what is going on in their organisation.

7. **Developmental orientation.** Someone who has experience of and takes a keen and active interest in others' development.

8. **Inventiveness.** Someone who is open to new ideas and to different ways of doing things; someone who perceives different and useful connections and patterns, and is a good, creative problem-solver in his/her own right.

(This list was developed by Dr Brian O'Neill.)

There are some interesting features in this list. The main one is the emphasis in the first three items on organisational issues. This was part of the rationale for adding the organisation base to the four-base approach in the mentoring wheel. Management perspective refers to the breadth of knowledge and understanding that the mentor is likely to be able to bring to the relationship. This works in a number of ways. First, for individuals in a Finance Department for example, it will give them a window on the world outside of their own function. They should gradually get some perspective on how a finance function fits in with other functions of the business. In other words, it gets them out of their own little corner and encourages them to look upwards and outwards. This should enrich their own understanding and approach. Secondly, they may be able to gain, almost by osmosis, some second-hand experience of this business or organisation and perhaps other businesses or organisations.

Organisational know-how contributes some knowledge of the particular political and cultural environment in which the learners work. As well as developing their own understanding of the way their organisation works, the know-how of the mentor can assist the learners in a practical way in terms of navigating them around the organisation. Mentors often have leverage or influence within the organisation, and this can help them to support the learners, for instance, in terms of negotiating or providing opportunities for learning at work. The credibility factor also contributes in this dimension.

These three factors, taken together, suggest a powerful package that mentors can bring to bear in support of, and on behalf of, their learners. And these features are highly valued by learners. It is also the case that, as often as not, these qualities do not need to be 'trained into' mentors because they arrive with them ready-made.

This should be a reassurance to potential mentors as it should convince them that they naturally have some of the most important qualities required.

Accessibility is not surprisingly always valued highly by learners. In the early stages of a mentor–learner relationship, this feature needs to be discussed and agreed upon in the terms of reference because it is possible, and perhaps even likely, that the learner wants or needs more time and attention than the mentor can offer.

The communication skills are an obvious must. It is rare for someone to volunteer for the mentoring role if he/she has not got at least a reasonable working level of communication skills. However, mentors are as likely to learn about their own repertoire of skills during the course of the relationship as the learner is. In this, as in all other cases, the mentors should not expect themselves to be perfect. As the saying goes, perfection takes a little longer. We all need to be aware that good enough is good enough.

The empowering orientation is perhaps no surprise either. Although it may seem not to bear an immediately obvious connection to the mentoring role, it does seem that the best mentors are those who default to giving a greater share of responsibility to the learner, where it is appropriate to do so. What really good mentors do is to gauge where the learner is able to cope, and to create the conditions in which the individual can safely push the boundaries a little bit without fear of failure.

Developmental orientation comes from people's experience and desire to bring others on. Good managers, who are natural mentors, usually have a long history of developing others and know the ropes in terms of how to do it. They generate a good deal of respect and trust from others by virtue of doing so. Like all of these skills and attributes, for some people they come quite naturally. For the rest of us, we have to work a little harder.

41

The inventiveness is an indication of the potential and the need for the mentor to be a creative problem-solver. This has two basic dimensions. One is the ability to suggest novel solutions to problems where the learner might get stuck. The other relates to the mentor's ability to guide the learner through a structured problem-solving process, like the one set out in Chapter 8. The added advantage of this is that the learner picks up on the problem-solving skill as he/she goes along.

The other dimension is based around the quality of flexibility and openness to new experiences. Inventive mentors are rarely lost for something to do, even in the most unusual circumstances. Neither are they stuck into inflexible and tram-line solutions or habits. As a mentor–learner relationship, like most effective working relationships, is a partnership, there has to be a component of mutual respect and mutual tolerance for different ways of going about things.

The individual skill areas associated with each of the four bases of the mentoring wheel are covered in the appropriate chapters.

However, we should be able to relate these qualities to behaviours. This will give us a better basis for self-assessment.

Below, we have returned to our list of key skills, qualities and attributes, and have summarised the positive indicators of each category.

1. Management perspective

- Has experience of management, usually at a senior level
- Has experience of working in varied organisations
- Has studied management issues
- Is used to working cross-functionally or in a consultancy capacity.

42

2. Organisational know-how

- Understands the organisational structure, its policies and procedures, and how the work and the workforce are organised
- Understands the cultural norms and values of the organisation, and knows how things are done
- Knows who to contact to get something done
- Is used to handling cross-departmental tasks, projects and relationships
- Keeps in touch with what is going on in the organisation.

3. Credibility

- Has developed the job and put his/her own mark on it; is widely seen as a competent performer
- Has a reputation in the organisation as a 'professional'; sets a good example – by not indulging in personal gossip, by maintaining a sensible distance from others in the organisation, by cooperating with other managers and departments, and by behaving ethically

- Has grown into the job by acquiring the full range of knowledge, abilities and skills required

- Has adapted his/her appearance, manner and 'public image' to be broadly compatible with the organisation's norms and values

- Has built bridges with boss, colleagues and other important people in the organisation.

4. Accessibility

- Makes time available when someone is in need, e.g. by staying on late at the office

- Keeps appointments

- Follows an open-door policy for much of the time

- Makes people feel their questions and concerns are important

- Treats others' intentions and priorities with respect, even when holding a contrary view.

43

5. Communication

- Expresses views and thoughts in a fluent and articulate manner; uses apt examples and metaphors to get the message across

- Adapts how he/she speaks to other people, e.g. uses technical expressions or specialist jargon only when they will be understood, and lengthy explanations only when they will be appreciated

- Asks insightful questions that enable the other person to get across what matters

- Checks frequently for understanding

- Promotes two-way communication

- Listens attentively and visibly, by doing things like maintaining eye-contact, and by confirming that he/she has understood.

6. Empowering orientation

- Creates a feeling of energy and excitement; encourages people from different departments or units to work together and to share information and ideas

- Allows people opportunity and latitude; having agreed objectives, encourages people to get on with it in the way they think best

- Enables subordinates to play a role in the organisation that challenges them, brings satisfaction and engages their commitment

- Publicises and takes satisfaction from the achievements of staff and colleagues.

7. Developmental orientation

- Provides opportunities for people to perform and achieve above and beyond their current levels and expectations

- Delegates responsibilities that are progressively more challenging and job enriching

- Invests personal time in developing subordinates

- Gives constructive feedback

- Invests time in contributing to in-company training events

- Selects and assigns task objectives so that, as well as contributing to the mission of the department, they are suitable learning opportunities for the subordinate.

8. Inventiveness

- Can usually find creative ways to circumvent or overcome obstacles

- Generates, examines and evaluates a broad range of options and alternatives

- Is a 'lateral thinker', i.e. is able to draw unusual connections and parallels, and can see useful associations and patterns in things

- Is an active supporter of good ideas in the workplace.

It would be a marvellous role model who could score ten out of ten on each of these qualities or the associated repertoire of skills. It is not necessary for us to be unrealistic in our choice of mentors. It shouldn't be treated as a wish list, which we use to eliminate all but the highest paragons of virtue. Mentoring is an additive model, and what we bring adds value to the activities of learners. But all of us have our own relative strengths and weaknesses. So how does a list like this have some practical uses? One way to use it is as a framework to think about mentoring. We need somewhere rational to start. Another way to use it is developmentally. In other words, we can use it to measure our own strengths and weaknesses, and therefore begin to be able to address them.

We can also use this list to begin to relate skills and qualities to a particular context or situation.For any particular context or relationship, of course, not all of the skills and qualities will be of equal weight. This will depend on the individual circumstances that pertain to the situation. We can use the considerations of the mentoring wheel to describe any particular context in some detail. From here, we can get a much clearer idea of the skill requirements and priorities. Let us look at a couple of contrasting examples.

45

■ CASE STUDY

Induction of graduates into an organisation

Organisation base

A major focus here. Graduates need to 'get to know the ropes'.

Context base

Newly recruited graduates. There is an induction agenda and programme, but very little by way of specified outputs from the mentoring relationship. The focus of the programme is more on information, awareness and understanding.

Development base

The graduates are likely to be confident learners, and there is no formal learning programme.

▶

Interpersonal base

Communication skills required to maintain the relationship. No special problems expected.

Style

The relationship needn't be too formal, but a business-like approach is expected and it is considered 'at work'. Some guidelines are issued, but there is no imposed structure to the relationship, although there is a structured process to the induction itself.

What we can deduce from this is that those qualities that operate mainly in the organisation base of the mentoring wheel will be prioritised very highly. With mature learners, and fairly modest learning requirements, the developmental orientation of the mentors need not be too high, although learners would be likely to favour someone who is used to and comfortable with developing young people. Less strong requirements in the context and interpersonal bases mean that the empowering orientation and inventiveness will be prioritised lower.

If we look at the weights of the relative requirements here we can see that:

1	Management perspective	*High. Role models required*
2	Organisational know-how	*Very high*
3	Credibility	*High*
4	Accessibility	*Medium*
5	Communication	*Medium*
6	Empowering orientation	*Low*
7	Developmental orientation	*Medium*
8	Inventiveness	*Low*

Let us go through this process for a mature woman who has just been promoted to a supervisor's job. Let us suppose she has a modest formal education, is perhaps lacking in some confidence, and is going through an extended management development programme. We can see that the profile will be quite different. Here the focus will be much more strongly on the context requirements (the management programme), and on the developmental and interpersonal bases.

1 Management perspective	*Medium / high*
2 Organisational know-how	*Low*
3 Credibility	*Low*
4 Accessibility	*Medium / high*
5 Communication	*High*
6 Empowering orientation	*High*
7 Developmental orientation	*High*
8 Inventiveness	*High*

47

This is a fairly systematic way of thinking about the requirements for particular mentoring contexts. Here is another approach:

■ CASE STUDY

A manager in a trust hospital

'I have chosen WD to be my personal mentor. My reasons for choosing her are threefold:

1. *I like and respect her, and I could not communicate honestly with someone I did not feel happy with.*

2. *I respect her role within the organisation and will not want to let her down. I am not good at self-discipline and the thought of*

▶

> *distance learning concerns me, as I do need driving. The thought of 'failing' in Wendy's eyes will encourage me and give me the motivation to succeed and do well.*
>
> *3. I will accept her advice and help (again something I'm not too good at). I will encourage her to push me and make me stick to the deadlines I set myself.*
>
> *WD and I have agreed to meet at least monthly initially. Throughout the course, I plan to call on other mentors as the need arises. KI has agreed to help me wherever and whenever he can. I will need help when I approach the finance workbook, and as I have little experience with technology, I'm sure I will be seeking help often. I have had training in 'Microsoft Word' and 'Excel' since the course started and this is my first effort!'*
>
> The version given by the potential learner is no less rational, and is also based on a clear understanding and appreciation of the personal qualities of the intended mentor. But viewing the selection issue from two perspectives gives us an indication that there is a question to be answered here.

48

Who should choose mentors?
■ ■ ■

In the case study above, the mentor was chosen because of her special qualities, which were known to the learner. There is always a vulnerability on behalf of the learner, and a high level of trust is required for the relationship to work well. This would suggest that it is important for the learner to be able to choose the mentor. Allowing a learner to choose their own mentor increases substantially the chances that the relationship will be productive and effective. It can also prevent problems.

■ CASE STUDY

Conflict in a mentoring relationship

'Ray and I didn't really get on from the beginning. Our styles were just too different. On the face of it, he had all of the qualifications for the job. He had been around for a while, and was well respected in his department. In fact, he was seen as a bit of a high flyer. But that was partly the problem. He treated our sessions as if they were just another project, and I was the subordinate who was supposed to deliver. He was always wanting quick results, and he pushed me pretty hard at times. When there were problems, I think he found it difficult to see why I was stuck – I just wasn't as confident or accomplished as he was, and he would take over and sort it out instead of giving me a bit of space to work it out for myself. In the end I realised that I was doing things his way, and for his benefit rather than for my own. When I eventually plucked up the courage to tackle him about it, he just didn't understand. I had to ask to change mentors in the end, and that upset him and me. It left a nasty taste really.'

49

But, of course, there are reasons why it is not possible or easy for learners to choose their own mentors. One of the most important reasons why learners can't choose their own mentors is because they may not know the potential mentors well enough to make an informed judgement. In the case of the London school children being paired with role models from a major bank, the mentors and the learners will know nothing of each other. In this case, a third party must coordinate the assignments. In general, there are very few ground rules that would enable the coordinator to do this in any systematic way. However, there may be some basis for doing it in a rational way. A few examples might include:

1 **Geographical.** Selection could be based on where learners and mentors live or work.

2 **Special need.** If any of the learners have special needs, the potential mentors could be polled about whether they have any interest or experience in that area.

3 **Life interests.** Mentors and learners could be asked to

declare some out-of-work interests, and pairings could be made on that basis.

4 **Vocational interest.** Learners could be given a briefing on the various operational or functional areas of the workplace or organisation, and they could select their own particular preference. They could then be assigned a mentor on that basis.

A similar set of criteria could be built for any context, with a little thought. However, even on an in-company programme the same situation might apply. This leads us on to the next reason why it might cause difficulties if learners have a free choice.

This is the question of availability of mentors. If an organisation has ten people willing to be mentors for ten learners, a free choice could lead to practical difficulties. The problem may even be exacerbated when the learners have some knowledge of the mentors. If all of the learners opt for one mentor, then the programme will be in difficulties from the outset. One possible way around this particular difficulty is to allow learners to find their own mentors, and only then train them.

The third reason for not allowing learners a completely free choice is when there is an organisational purpose that influences the pairing of mentors and learners. If, for instance, an organisation has set up a mentoring scheme explicitly to foster a cross-departmental awareness and communication, then a free choice of mentors within departments would be inappropriate.

Where mentors are assigned, there is always a danger that things will not work out well, as the case study above demonstrates. Experience shows that there are usually two kinds of reason for things going wrong. The first is interpersonal – the chemistry is somehow wrong. The second reason is usually to do with confusing the mentoring and the normal work contexts. This normally happens when the mentor takes too strong a control of the relationship, and defines the standards without treating the relationship as 'off-line'.

Such a situation is unlikely to occur in a one-off relationship or in natural mentoring relationships, where the learner chooses the mentor. However, it can happen in a scheme or programme where the learners are assigned to mentors. In these circumstances, the programme should have provision for mutual opt-out of the relationship. There should be some monitoring of the relationship by a third party – for example, a coordinator or programme manager – to pick up potential problems. Neither should all of the attention be on the learner. Mentors, too, need to have access to sources of advice and support.

Should line managers be mentors?
■ ■ ■

This is a vexed question and there is no definitive answer. On the one hand, good managers are, almost by definition, good natural mentors. They will be used to developing people and engaging them respectfully as human beings. The natural line manager-mentors are also easy to spot. When a learner, given a free choice of mentor, asks for his/her line manager, you know that this is a supportive individual with all of the requisite skills.

51

It is also somewhat difficult to answer such a question in principle without knowing the individuals involved, and without knowing the particular context. If a manager has encouraged a subordinate to go on an external course, and he/she wants some support, it may be quite natural for him/her to ask the line manager. In that case, the line manager will quite likely make a good job of the mentoring. It would also have the added benefit of cementing and strengthening their working relationship.

But many learners fail to recognise that they can have the support and involvement of their line manager and an off-line mentor as well. All of the mentoring input does not have to be invested in a single individual. If the individuals are interested in learning (and we expect that they are), then they have everything to gain from the extra insights and different approaches that they are likely to see from another individual.

What should not happen is that the learner is assigned to his/her line manager as a mentor in a programme or context that is different from the normal operational responsibilities. The reason for this is that the responsibilities of the line manager as a mentor and as a line manager can easily conflict. Confidentiality is just one issue that can inhibit the relationship. If the learner has not chosen the line manager but has been assigned to one, then the relationship is line manager–subordinate, and needs to be treated honestly as such.

Training mentors
■ ■ ■

Although some organisations train mentors to build a team which can later mentor if required, it is more usually the case that mentors are selected and then trained. How should we go about training mentors?

As always, this depends on the context. In a quite literal sense, if the context is complicated, then mentors may need quite detailed training on the requirements. In the case of management NVQs, mentors need training in the particular assessment requirements of the programme. This is not just for the sake of the learner. Mentors themselves will need to feel comfortable in answering questions and offering advice. In some schemes, the assessment requirements are so daunting for the mentors that separate, expert advice and support are provided, while the mentors provide the interpersonal needs and the process facilitation. However detailed the context requirements, mentors need a briefing so that they understand the basic dimensions of the important criteria.

The training needs of the mentors can be analysed by using the four bases of the mentoring wheel. Training needs usually fall into the following categories:

Mentoring skills and processes

Do the mentors:

- Understand what mentoring is about?

- Know about the separate roles involved?

- Know about process facilitation?

Interpersonal and communication skills

Do the mentors:

- Understand and use counselling skills?

- Listen as well as tell?

- Use appropriate questioning skills?

- Have empathy?

- Make good, effective working relationships?

Learning and development

Do the mentors:

- Have a developmental orientation?

- Understand the learning cycle?

- Have coaching skills?

- Respect other learning styles?

53

These kinds of question provide not only the diagnostic, but also the agenda for any training that is necessary. If mentors are selected for their skills, attributes and for having appropriate experience, then the training needs can be quite minimal. However, it should be borne in mind that most mentors need some intervention. One half of that should be about information – the requirements of the role and the particular context. The other half should be an opportunity for reflection and orientation. Prospective mentors value the opportunity to discuss and prepare themselves. They usually need the chance to ask questions and swop ideas to prepare themselves.

■ *Mentoring action points*

If you are about to be a mentor :

- Make sure that you become familiarised with the context, the processes and the criteria that will operate

- Use the list of qualities and the role descriptions of the mentoring wheel to assess your own strengths and weaknesses

- Discuss these matters and your mutual expectations with your prospective learner.

'[Mentors] ... no one can get anywhere without one.'

Sir John Harvey Jones

Chapter 4

■ ■ ■

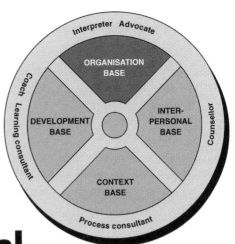

The organisational perspective

■ *Key learning points*

1 The organisational perspective will be represented in the organisation base of the mentoring wheel.

2 There are various ways that the influence and interests of an organisation can be present in a mentoring scheme or individual relationship.

3 The culture and the organisational readiness to change can be an important influence in mentoring.

4 The roles of interpreter and advocate can be defined as the positional strength of the mentor.

> **■ CASE STUDY**
>
> ## PG – Marketing manager
>
> *'My most formative experience of mentoring comes from what I call negative mentoring – the manager who is everything you aspire not to be and you therefore work doubly hard to ensure you are not like them when you become a manager.*
>
> *For instance, they never have time for you – you will therefore bend over backwards to have time for everyone for whom you are a manager.*
>
> *They never advocate or support training/operational development – you therefore work harder to ensure that your staff in the future have every chance to receive training.*
>
> *They never give advice or an answer – so you try extra hard to advise, encourage, counsel, etc, and always give an answer, even if it is "I don't know but I'll find out".*
>
> *They don't believe in appraisals – you therefore put a tremendous amount of effort into appraisals in the future.*
>
> *All of this is as a result of the knowledge that you personally missed out on a lot!'*

The organisation base of the mentoring wheel represents the interests of, and the influence of, the organisation over mentoring relationships. It also relates to the position, expertise and perspective of the individual mentors in relation to the organisation.

It is one of the major ways that mentoring is different from counselling. Counselling focuses almost purely on the relationship between counsellor and counsellee. In mentoring, there is usually some application (represented by the context base) that surrounds the relationship, and influences it. Because we are concerned not only with mentoring in work-based situations, but also with mentoring in a managerial context, the influence of the organisation has to be taken into account.

There is a number of options or different ways in which the organisational perspective can be represented in a mentoring relationship or scheme. The two basic dimensions are:

■ Individual relationship versus corporate scheme

■ Internal versus external mentors.

Individual relationship versus corporate scheme
■ ■ ■

In many programmes the mentoring is sponsored by the organisation. In these cases, there is a scheme or an initiative which is driven by the organisation for its own needs. In such cases, the objectives of the organisation will be present as part of the context of the mentoring relationship. These influences can be shown as in Figure 4.

59

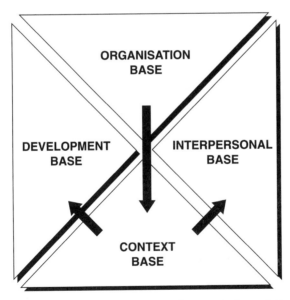

Fig 4 Organisational objectives affect the mentoring relationship

What this means is that the relationship will not be totally self-contained and introspective. There will be some broader purpose, and maybe even some quite specific objectives. However, we shouldn't suggest that this will provide a constraint or a 'dead hand' on the relationship. Usually, the purposes and motives for in-company schemes are enabling, developmental and positive. Where they are more to do with control or policing they almost inevitably inhibit a productive relationship.

■ CASE STUDY

AC – a housing manager

'When we started the Diploma programme our directors decided they wanted to be our mentors. There was no free choice, they just decided to mentor us. Now I don't like her as my line manager, so it was never going to work as a real and trusting relationship. I didn't think she had the right skills or approach, and she also did-n't understand as much as I did about the details of the pro-gramme.

She treated our sessions as she would any other task – that is, she was more concerned with getting it done at all costs, never mind the development part. What really made me fed up, though, was that it was written into my key objectives for this year, and the expectation was unrealistic – there was no way I could complete it by the end of the year.

In the end it just became a battle. It wasn't mentoring at all – in fact it wasn't even good management, to be honest.'

This case study demonstrates the sort of thing that can happen if the organisation (via its agents, the managers) puts too heavy or inappropriate requirements on learners, apparently for the good of the organisation. You can't help feeling that this is also more for the good of the individual 'mentors' than it is for the learners.

The guidelines for setting up and conducting a good in-company programme we will save for Chapter 10, although we can take some strong hints from experiences like those found in the case study above. In good programmes, there will be objectives and purposes. Although these will be represented in the context description, nonetheless there is still an organisational or cultur-al overlay that influences the individual mentoring relationships.

In other cases, the relationships arise from individual initiative or need, rather than from corporate planning. The most obvious version of this is the development of natural mentoring relationships, as discussed earlier. However, it can also arise from a learner being supported in some external programme.

We can summarise the issues and choices as follows:

Corporate schemes

Advantages

- They tend to be planned and structured
- The mentors are likely to be selected, briefed or trained
- They are likely to offer a balance of corporate and individual benefits
- They are likely to be well resourced
- They are likely to offer leverage or an opportunity at work.

Disadvantages

- Where line managers are mentors, the roles or interests may conflict
- Corporate interests may override individual interest
- Mentors may be conscripted and less committed
- Learners may not be able to choose mentors.

Individual mentors

Advantages

- Mentors are likely to be chosen for their individual qualities
- The focus is individual not corporate

61

- There are few constraints on the relationship

- Mentoring will be relationship and not task-focused.

Disadvantages

- Mentors may not be trained

- Mentors may have little leverage or influence

- Development may be less work-related

- There may be little support or recognition for the relationship.

Internal versus external mentors
■ ■ ■

The other basic dimension is whether the mentor is internal or external to the organisation. Where the mentor is external to the organisation the situation can be more difficult, because in those circumstances the mentor does not represent directly the interests of the organisation. He or she is not the agent of the organisation in that sense. This brings advantages and disadvantages.

The advantage is that the terms of reference of the relationship are basically internal to that relationship, and the only needs to be satisfied are those of the individual. However, there can be exceptions to this. For instance, an organisation might set up a mentoring scheme with external mentoring support. In such cases, the question shifts to how the interests of the organisation are represented. Who sets the outcomes? What are the reporting or information requirements?

The disadvantage is that the mentor in those circumstances is less likely to have influence or detailed knowledge of the organisation. It, therefore, may be more difficult for the mentor to be an advocate or opportunity provider, because he/she does not have direct leverage within the organisation.

The influence of organisational culture
■ ■ ■

Where organisations have opted positively for a mentoring approach, and support mentoring activity and initiatives, there are many aspects of the interests and nature of that organisation that will affect the mentoring relationships. These usually manifest themselves in two basic areas of influence:

- **Organisational objectives.** These will influence the existence of the mentoring relationships (whether they exist at all), and they will influence the structures and systems that surround the mentoring initiative. However, for most practical purposes, these will be represented in the description and constraints of the context base of the mentoring wheel (see page 77). Both for the organisation and for the mentors, proper analysis and action of this organisation base will enable them to be dealt with appropriately.

63

- **Organisational culture.** This will influence the mentoring relationships within an organisation and it must be 'read', understood and dealt with in order for the relationships to be productive.

What is culture?
■ ■ ■

Culture is a concept that is central not only to the way an organisation operates, but to the success it can expect to achieve. Further, we know that culture influences an organisation's ability to respond to change.

Peters and Waterman, in their seminal study *In Search of Excellence* (Harper & Row, New York, 1982) studied the attributes of successful organisations. One of their discoveries was that successful organisations had, believed in and acted upon a strong cultural base.

> Without exception, the dominance and coherence of culture proved to be an essential quality of the excellent companies. In these companies, people way down the line knew what they were supposed to

do in most situations because the handful of guiding values is crystal clear, the shared values in the excellent companies are clear, in large measure because the mythology is rich.

Culture is difficult to articulate and define precisely, but it appears to involve a shared set of basic assumptions, habits, approaches and values. It arises from a wide variety of influences, from the nature of the business activity, the external environment and the national culture to the visions of its leaders.

Although very little is understood about the 'science of culture' at the moment, a good deal of the research so far undertaken suggests that culture has an important influence over many aspects of an organisation's activities. However, even if it is difficult to describe scientifically, common sense and personal experience demonstrate that culture can be easily identified. We know, for example, that it influences relationships, the way things are done, productivity, and so on.

Why is culture important?
■ ■ ■

Organisational culture is important because it has a pervasive influence over all relationships within that organisation. It affects status, conduct, and perceived importance of mentors. In particular, there are some aspects of mentoring relationships that interact directly with the culture.

1 Mentoring relationships are about developing people, increasing capability and therefore empowering people.

2 The 'host' organisation may have to accept that it has very little direct control on these relationships – unlike normal line relationships.

3 Mentoring relationships are about change. In the first instance, they involve change for the individuals concerned, but they can and do impact on wider changes within the organisation. The organisation may welcome these, or it may be surprised by them. Therefore it may or may not be ready, and it may or may not be willing and cooperative.

4 Exact outcomes may be difficult to predict or prescribe. Therefore an organisation often has to be able to cope with the
ambiguity or uncertainty of the outputs or consequences of
mentoring relationships within the organisation.

What this means in practice is that some organisations are better disposed to supporting mentoring relationships by virtue of
their culture. It is not just the mentoring relationships themselves that are, or are not, supported. In fact, they often are. But
problems can arise because the nature of the relationships is
counter-cultural within the organisation. Also, when learners
start to become more capable and empowered, and when they
start to 'flex' their new-found learning and competence, or when
they begin to question the systems and processes within the
organisation, it can become uncomfortable for the organisation
involved.

This is when the organisation, to protect the *status quo*, starts to
put up blocks and barriers to change. These blocks and barriers
can take many forms, but they often involve shifting the focus
from the innovative, creative, strategic, or long-term to the
parochial, short-term, tactical (rather than strategic), and
urgent (rather than important). These are often coupled with the
talking down of new ideas and a focus on personality and power
rather than on business issues.

65

Because so many mentoring relationships and schemes have
change – both individual and organisational – as their primary
purpose, an organisation needs to have a culture which will support and accommodate change in a positive way. Not surprisingly, a strong culture and a strong orientation to change tend to go
together. Some of the key characteristics of strong change organisations are the following:

Open organisation structures

- Few layers
- Flexible and permeable boundaries
- Cross-departmental communication and team activity

- Devolved decision-making
- Hierarchy does not inhibit flow of ideas.

Open communication

- Shared and well-communicated vision
- The exchange of information is encouraged
- Commitment and participation is sought
- Selling more than telling.

Innovative values

- New ideas are respected
- Change is seen as healthy
- There is cooperation between business units
- Mistakes are tolerated.

Top management support for change

- Enabling vision
- Consistency of purpose and goals
- Change is rewarded
- Sensible risks are accepted
- Authority as well as responsibility is delegated.

Management systems

- There are robust and accepted decision-making processes
- Training is widely used
- Performance is related to reward.

Supportive management

- Managers are open-minded and flexible

- Managers are also leaders who motivate

- Staff are encouraged to contribute.

Allocation of resources and responsibility

- Development projects are resourced

- Time to improve products and services is encouraged

- Managers can think forward as well as fight fires

- Changes are planned and resourced.

Systematic management of ideas

- Staff are encouraged to keep up-dated

- Suggestions are encouraged and welcomed

- Quality customer and market information is sought.

(Adapted from Brian O'Neill, *The Organisation Change Inventory, Managing in Context*, IM.)

In order to clear up some of the complexities and ambiguities, we should here look at what a mentor might bring in relation to the organisation base of the mentoring wheel. We can use the model to describe some of the issues and the priorities involved.

Let us look first at the role-model descriptions. The role models in this base of the mentoring wheel are those of:

- **Interpreter.** This is someone who will deepen your knowledge of your own and other organisations, and who will help a learner to make sense of how the bits of the jigsaw fit together.

- **Advocate.** This is someone who will negotiate and operate on the learner's behalf, for his/her benefit.

67

The role of interpreter
■ ■ ■

In Chapter 3, we looked at the qualities that we would ideally like a mentor to possess. What mentors bring to a relationship with respect to the interpreter's role is their management perspective. This may be gained in a number of ways. It may be gained by direct management experience. Mentors, by virtue of their seniority and breadth of experience, tend to 'know the ropes' more than most. Their experience may also be gained by working with managers in organisations in a consultancy or service role. Human resource professionals, for instance, often have wide experience of management practice and pressures, particularly if they have a training or development role.

The scope of a mentor's experience is also important here. Mentors may have more cross-functional understanding than the average learner, by virtue of working across departments or by working at a level senior enough that they have direct cross-functional experience, and they understand how departments relate to each other, and how the different departments and functions contribute to the business. They may also have experience of how other organisations work – the different systems, processes, and cultures.

If the mentors are external, they are likely to have a more general experience of management and more experience of other organisations, which may balance their lack of detailed knowledge of any particular organisation.

The good news, then, is that if mentors are selected properly, they are likely to have a good mix of these qualities and experiences. They can then act as interpreters and guides into the ways of the world with a perspective that the learner alone may not have. They do this by knowing or predicting how things get done, how systems and processes work, and by helping learners to understand how their activities contribute to the organisation as a whole. They can also assist the learner in thinking about the next step, in terms of seniority or responsibility.

The role of advocate
■　■　■

To be a good advocate for a learner, a mentor needs a combination of the following:

- **Organisational know-how.** This comes from experience. It involves knowing how to get things done and how things work. It also involves knowing and being fluent with the culture, and understanding the power structure (both formal and informal) within an organisation. This is slightly more difficult for an external mentor. However, they may be able to contribute here by having that general knowledge and understanding of the way that organisations work.

- **Credibility or influence.** The mentor will enjoy personal and professional credibility. This may come from known achievement, position or expertise within the organisation itself. Alternatively, it may come by virtue of being a respected external consultant or expert.

Being an advocate usually involves a combination of harder and softer priorities. The softer one involves creating the right atmosphere and attitude to the work and the development the learner is undertaking. In this case, the more senior the mentor championing the learner, the better. It gives an important sign and symbol to the rest of the organisation that what they are doing is significant and important. It creates respect for the undertaking. It also legitimises and alerts people to the fact that the learner is doing something out of the run of the mill in terms of work-based tasks. This, in turn, should create a cocoon which protects the activity of the learner and enables people to think of it in a positive light.

The harder priority is that the mentor can operate as an *opportunity provider* on behalf of the learner.

■ CASE STUDY

Competent Manager Programme

In the Institute of Management Certificate in Management programmes, the learners have to demonstrate competence in the units and elements of the MCI Occupational Standards for Management. Among these are the requirement to:

- Lead a meeting or group discussion

- Counsel staff

- Recruit staff, or demonstrate competence of recruitment processes

- Hold a budget, or monitor the use of resources.

For most candidates on the development programme, it is quite common that there are at least one or two of these requirements that they do not do as part of their job description. An analysis of their development needs identifies that they need opportunities to develop and demonstrate these competencies.

Mentors are very good at helping to create work-based opportunities for learners to 'have a go' for themselves. In order for them to do this, the mentors need to be fairly well-placed or influential within the organisation so that they can negotiate on behalf of the learners or support them in their own efforts.

The role of advocate usually involves communication with the line manager of the learner. A good suggestion is that, in the early part of the relationship, the mentor or learner initiates a tripartite discussion with the line manager, as shown in Figure 5.

The discussion can be used to try to get the line manager 'on side' with the needs and aspirations of the learner. It is also a chance to gauge if the line manager is likely to be enabling or inhibiting the needs of the learner. Although much of the discussion will be about communicating information, it is also an opportunity to influence and negotiate.

The following are the sort of items that might be worth discussing:

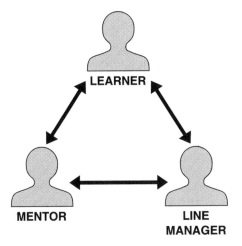

Fig 5 Tripartite communication model

71

Tripartite meeting – agenda

- Introductions and 'get to know you'
- Discussion and clarification of roles
- Terms of reference
- Assessment/discussion of needs
- Planning of time/activities
- Questions/issues.

The mentor as a role model
■ ■ ■

Mentors will be successful in the organisation base roles if they act as role models for the learner. In all of the anecdotal evidence about 'natural' mentors, this role-modelling aspect of the job comes out very strongly. It takes a number of forms. One form it takes is that of admiration for the position, seniority or achievements of the mentor. Another form is that of the mentor's personal approach or style.

Within the mentoring relationship there are some specific and functional reasons for the learner to role model the mentor. These can be summarised by saying that the mentor is likely to have a set of habits, approaches, tools and skills that will benefit the learner. Further, in the course of the relationship the learner is likely to be able to see at first hand how the mentor uses his/her skills. Good, positive experience has a way of transmitting to those who see it and experience it, and this can only benefit the learner. Some examples are:

- **Project management.** A mentor will often have mastered the management cycle of plan, action, review to a greater extent than the learner.

- **Setting goals.** If a mentor is good at setting goals and monitoring progress towards their achievement, then the learner is likely to gain the habit and the skill.

- **Time management.** Mentors will rarely be able to devote unlimited time to learners. Meetings will have to be planned and scheduled. If they take place in working time and in the working environment, they will have to be time-managed. As mentors, we do our learners a favour by using the time productively and starting and finishing according to schedule.

- **Behaviour/style.** Sometimes, this is the biggest revelation or contribution that mentors can make to the development of a learner. When learners see how mentors cope and go about their business – particularly in relation to interpersonal relationships – it can open their eyes to possibilities of alternative ways of doing things. This can relate to coping, managing stress, or to dealing with different kinds of situation or different types of approach from other people.

A good way of summing up these roles, and either communicating with or training mentors, is to use the term *positional strength*. The relative positional strength of the mentor is the extent to which he/she can satisfy the requirements of the roles that we have set out here.

Positional strength can be defined by:

- The mentor's influence over others within the organisation

- The mentor's understanding of the key issues in departments/business units across the organisation

- The mentor's understanding of the culture and power structures within the organisation

- Whether the mentor is perceived as a leader or expert, or as influential by peers and colleagues

- Whether the mentor has access to resources

- Whether the mentor is a senior manager or has influence with top management

- Whether the mentor is involved in major changes or initiatives

- Whether the mentor knows what is going on.

■ *Skillcheck*

For the organisation base of the mentoring wheel, the skills required by mentors are of a quite different order than those of the other bases. It is important to take account of the organisational environment in which the mentoring takes place. The mentoring will be supported and productive only to the extent that it fits in with the interests, habits and approaches of the organisation. In short, the culture will be an influence. Where the mentoring is part of a corporate scheme the *organisational readiness*, which is influenced by the openness to and ability to manage change, is a vital factor.

For the individual mentors, their perspective, influence and functional or technical expertise can be described by their *positional strength*.

The roles of interpreter, advocate and role model will be associated with some quite 'difficult' skills like:

- Negotiation

- Influence

- Goal setting

- Time management.

The associated qualities will be around:

- Respect

- Self-confidence

- Authority.

'Mentoring schemes are one important way of giving boys role models and a sense of what they can achieve.'

David Blunkett MP

Chapter 5

■ ■ ■

The uses of mentoring

■ **Key learning points**

1 The context base of mentoring describes the particular set of purposes that surround a mentoring relationship.

2 These purposes or applications can have an astonishing variety.

3 Applications can be classified according to their major focus in the four bases.

4 The major role model in this base is that of process consultant.

In this chapter we will be looking at the context base of the mentoring wheel. The context base involves the precise set of purposes and structures that surround any particular relationship. This makes it quite difficult to discuss, in a sense, because every programme or application will be different. We can get the flavour of what kind of differences or similarities there are if we look at a few diverse examples.

Here are some examples of organisations which have gone down the mentoring route:

The Library and Information Service (LIS)

There has been interest in the LIS nationwide in the efficacy of mentoring in professional development for many years. The British Library Research and Development Department has awarded a grant to the University of Central England to look at mentoring in the LIS community. Biddy Fisher has produced a training guide for mentoring for the Library Association. Mentoring was a key focus of the Library Association national conference.

Bank and school

School children in inner-city schools in a London borough are being paired with mentors from a major bank. The school children receive an orientation to work and a working environment, as well as support and encouragement in achieving good results.

British Alcan

British Alcan use mentoring widely, for diverse groups such as graduates, potential high-fliers and senior managers on MBA programmes.

British Gas

British Gas runs a mentoring scheme to help graduates who

78

make frequent job moves in the first few years of their development. The mentor is a key link between learner, line management and the training department. The relationships operate according to guidelines which cover frequency and reciprocal commitments.

Brent Council

Brent Council uses mentoring to aid the development of female middle managers into more senior roles. Male senior managers mentor female managers in a bid to break down barriers to progression.

TSB Bank

Mentoring is involved in many management development processes. It has been useful particularly in supporting self-managed learning.

79

AMI Healthcare

AMI Healthcare have introduced a mentoring scheme for senior managers on an executive development programme. Mentors support project work for areas unfamiliar to the learner.

We can also look in more detail at a few particular examples:

■ CASE STUDY

Affirmative action, mentoring and the emergence of cultural diversity in the USA

In the USA, there is an unparalleled number of mentoring programmes. Hundreds of highly successful programmes have been developed which positively influence equal opportunities and affirmative action for minority groups.

'The application of mentoring in providing a larger pool of high-potential youths to the future workforce and enhancing the potential of individuals already in the workforce has proven to be a low-cost, high-yield solution that pays off.'

▶

Although often funded and coordinated by corporate America or private foundations, many of these are volunteer programmes. Limited time and social distance do not make such programmes easy, but these programmes are making a huge difference in helping young people to cope.

Similar programmes are operating in the UK. An example is the Derby mentoring project, which seeks to use mentors to support Afro-Caribbean students in college.

(Based on an article in Empower magazine)

■ Key learning point

Mentoring programmes can have wide and ambitious social and cross-organisational functions.

■ CASE STUDY

National Mentoring Consortium
Source: *People Management*, September 1995

The National Mentoring Consortium aims to bridge the gap between university and employment by giving ethnic minority students the chance to develop their professional skills. One aim is to match students and mentors in appropriate career areas. The scheme also offers informal role models and contacts – not always easy for black students, as they are under-represented, particularly in senior positions. The project grew out of contacts and links with local companies and the University of East London. Norman McLean (director) explains how students reacted very positively to visits and discussions. In 1992 they found mentors for thirty students. Twenty-five employers were able to provide fifty black professionals to act as mentors. They found that the mentoring partnership was successful in more than 80 per cent of cases. Results were that 70 per cent said it boosted their confidence, 85 per cent reported greater awareness of the business world and 30 per cent said their academic work had improved – the latter was an unplanned bonus.

▶

The scheme has now been expanded to over 400 participants nationwide. The aim is not about promising a job, but about gaining insight into the work environment and providing role models.

■ Key learning point

Programmes aimed at a particular set of objectives (e.g. awareness of the business world) often have additional spin-off benefits, such as increased confidence and improved academic work.

■ CASE STUDY

Mentoring for international managers

Mentoring could be an important means of support to assist expatriate managers in settling into new assignments abroad. This is the conclusion of Christopher Conway and Kevin Barham, researchers from Ashridge Management College, as reported in the *Sunday Times*.

They suggest that mentoring can help managers who have to change their frame of reference quickly to become sensitised to the cultures they work in. Organisations can fail to appreciate how difficult it is for managers to make this kind of switch. These managers need to meet the direct challenge of the new job, but also to retain perspective for the wider organisation which in itself needs time for reflection and learning.

They report that some leading international companies are now incorporating mentors into their development for international managers. This assists them, not only to cope with their own changing situations, but to drive change throughout their organisations.

As well as benefiting the managers, the mentors themselves benefit.

'Mentoring is a two-way street. It really is a consciousness-raising relationship in which each party learns and grows', says Conway.

81

■ *Key learning points*

The detail in this particular case study is very interesting and informative. Some points worth mentioning are:

■ Learning has taken place on three levels – the challenge of the job, learning for the future and helping the organisation to learn. This demonstrates the complexity and depth of learning that can occur.

■ The role of the mentor can help managers to reflect on what they are doing.

■ The role of the mentor can help new staff to decode the organisation.

■ The private and personal nature of many of the mentoring relationships is evident.

■ There are numerous benefits for the mentors themselves.

The dimensions of mentoring relationships
■ ■ ■

These key points and other dimensions of the mentoring relationship are quite typical and appear in many of the applications – almost regardless of their particular contextual nature. This is useful to know, of course, but we also need to consider those ways in which one mentoring programme or relationship can be different from another. There are a number of dimensions that we can examine which will 'fix' a programme or relationship. The value of this is that it will enable us to build a picture and thus describe the key factors that might need to be taken into account in any particular context.

The various dimensions are:

1 Formal or informal

2 Structured or open-frame (natural) mentoring

3 Assigned or self-selected mentors.

Formal or informal

Quite often the mentor will have been appointed or selected either by the learner or by the organisation. The formal nature of this arrangement should not be mistaken for formality in style. The explicit process, purpose or agenda of the mentoring relationship may be formally structured, but the style or ethos of the relationship may be quite laid-back.

The informal mentoring relationship is one that arises quite naturally in the course of events. Neither the mentor nor learner may consider themselves as actually being in a mentor–learner relationship. In these cases, the mentor may not even know that that is what he/she is doing. Nonetheless many of the same processes and skills will be happening.

The core conditions for such relationships are quite simple: mutual interest; good communication skills; time; a lack of rules. However, there are other features that also seem to arise in many of these informal relationships. The lack of positioning for 'political' or petty organisational purposes is often cited as a refreshing difference from normal working contacts. The highly individual and intimate nature of the relationship is also often cited as a meaningful and valuable characteristic.

These sorts of feature and characteristic seem to develop easily and naturally in informal relationships. However, we should make a distinction between the genesis of a mentoring relationship and the style of it. Most natural mentoring relationships are fairly informal, although they can include a 'business-like' element in varying degrees. Equally, just because a relationship has begun because a learner is assigned to a mentor in a structured programme, does not mean that the relationship cannot be developed informally.

Structured or open-framed (natural) mentoring

Structured relationships usually apply where there is some systematic development programme or process involved. This may be a learning programme with defined outcomes and possibly even accreditation. It could also be a process like induction where the outcomes are less specific but just as important.

Open-framed relationships can be formal or informal. In other words, they may involve the explicit appointment of a mentor and a structured timetable, but they can also be free-wheeling and unbounded by specific objectives. They often derive from one person's need for support or even from a chance to chat now and then as the need arises.

Assigned or self-selected mentors

Another dimension of the mentoring relationship is who chooses the mentor? Clearly, in natural mentoring relationships, the route is mutual self-selection. In other contexts, however, the learner will be asked to select a mentor. This can happen either by the learner selecting a mentor who is then trained or briefed for the job, or by the learner selecting from a cohort of potential mentors.

In some schemes mentors are assigned without choice. Although this can work well, it is introducing a potential difficulty if the mentor and learner do not gel. One circumstance where the appointment of a mentor might be justified is where the learners do not know the potential mentors. In this case, it is a question of 'suck it and see'. Provision needs to be made for choices to be reviewed or changed if they are not working on either side.

Experience shows that a of lack of choice can be detrimental to the mentoring process. If it is not possible to offer learners a choice then, at a minimum, a veto should be offered.

All of these factors will influence the nature of the relationship and, in turn, the context of the relationship will influence some of these factors. The specific purposes or objectives might have a number of sources or points of focus.

The points of focus within the four-base model
■ ■ ■

One way of defining the application of a mentoring relationship is to examine the relative points of focus in the separate bases of the mentoring wheel. One of the advantages of the wheel is that it enables us to distinguish between the different types of mentoring relationship and, where necessary, between different mentoring programmes, on the basis of its primary purposes and aims.

All programmes have connections in each of the bases, but there is often a dominant base apparent for many relationships or programmes. We can look at each of the bases in turn.

The organisation base

Where a mentoring programme operates within an organisation there will be some organisational objectives that drive the mentor–learner relationship. In circumstances where the organisation doesn't 'own' or 'drive' a particular programme, the organisational objectives will still influence the nature of the relationship. Where the relationship arises out of a systematic programme initiated by that organisation, that programme will reflect, to a great extent, the objectives of the organisation.

From the organisational perspective, the issues that affect the relationship are as follows:

- The credibility of the programme
- The credibility of the mentors
- The culture of the organisation
- The commitment of the organisation
- The expertise of the mentors.

Organisationally focused mentor–learner relationships tend to focus on performance, efficiency, objectives and other operational issues.

Mentoring relationships that focus on the so-called *career functions* operate mainly in this base. They include any applications that involve career progression or development within a particular job role or integration into a particular organisational context. Examples include:

85

- Induction

- Role modelling

- Transmitting culture

- Developing expertise.

The context base

Mentoring relationships that focus in this base are bounded by a very particular set of requirements and objectives. Although they may be influenced or driven by organisational needs, they have a set of objectives which are totally internal to the mentoring programme in question.

A good example of programmes that concentrate on this particular context are Certificated Learning Programmes. Such programmes usually include specified processes or activities, such as workbooks, workshops, and so on. There are also specified outputs such as assignments and portfolios.

If such a programme has a component of self-study or self-directed learning, then there is usually some kind of support for the learner. This person may not always be called a mentor, but that is, in effect, what he/she is. In NVQ programmes, and specially in higher level NVQs such as management NVQs, mentor support is a specified requirement. In these cases, the particular requirements of the programme are likely to be the major focus for the learner.

As an example, on the Institute of Management Competent Manager Programme one of the major assessment processes is the collecting of evidence of competence for the NVQ Level 4 award. This means of assessment is quite unfamiliar to most people and quite unusual. Although it is basically a simple idea, it can become quite difficult and complex in the detail. For example, candidates have to:

- Address the individual elements of competence and associated performance criteria in a written document called a storyboard

- Collect relevant primary evidence from the workplace and get this supported by testimony

- Index, annotate and describe the evidence

- Relate the evidence to the standards via a matrix

- Reflect on their own practice and learning in relation to this element.

It can be quite a formidable set of tasks for a candidate. Anyone on such a programme will happily agree that the context provides the primary focus of his/her attention. It must also provide a major focus for the mentor–learner relationship. Candidates can be quite daunted by the requirements. They need a great deal of advice and support from the mentors, as the assessment looms large in their thoughts.

Mentors, too, can be daunted by these requirements. They have their own vulnerabilities and often need to feel that they should be 'one step ahead' of the learner-candidates. It is not actually necessary that they know more than the candidates about the assessment procedures and requirements, but they are only human, and they need to know at least as much as will enable them to feel comfortable and confident in advising and supporting the learner-candidate.

There are three basic options when it comes to supporting candidates in their needs:

1 Train the mentors so that they know at least as much as the candidates.

2 Provide external support for the assessment part of the programme, and leave the mentors to look after the other three bases. In this case the mentors may only need a briefing in order to have an overview or broad-brush picture of the requirements.

3 Train the mentors as process consultants so that they can take an active and positive role without having to know more than the learners. In this case, they are likely to need a briefing, as in option 2.

In practice, it is often the case that a hybrid approach is taken, mixing various of these options. But the point about the potential vulnerability of mentors in relation to the context base should be borne in mind. We will return to this point when we discuss the selection and training of mentors.

Examples of mentoring relationships in this base include:

- NVQ programmes

- Students at college or university

- Managers on MBA programmes.

The development base

In mentoring relationships for which this is the primary focus, the main area of concern is learning and learning processes. The learners will need to:

- Set learning objectives

- Monitor their own learning

- Understand learning processes.

Needless to say, the mentor needs to be equipped, and therefore comfortable, in supporting the learner in all of these. Examples include:

- Learning sets

- Peer mentoring.

The interpersonal base

Relationship-based mentor–learner relationships are those whose main area of concern is the well-being of the individual involved. This is a purely supportive function. Relationships in this base tend to have very little in terms of external requirements placed on them. The outcomes are those defined solely from point of view of the individual learner.

In such cases the mentor may be external to the organisation itself, although he/she is still likely to bring knowledge of a general business perspective to the relationship. However, it is also often useful if the mentor can begin to understand the organisational context in which the learner operates. This is saying nothing more than that, even where a relationship focuses in a particular base, the mentors need to acquaint themselves with the context and requirements of each of the other bases.

Unlike the career functions, the focus in the interpersonal base is the so-called *psychosocial functions*. These relate much more to the individual's values, motives and behaviour than to his/her ability to perform certain tasks. Examples include:

- Counselling

- Friendship.

It is quite rare for a mentoring relationship to be located uniquely in any one of the four bases at the expense of others. There is, however, quite often a primary focus in one of the bases. This does not mean that the others can be ignored or that they have any less importance. We have already stressed that when training or briefing mentors and prior to selecting mentors, potential mentors should be made aware of the requirements of all four of the bases.

89

Further applications
■ ■ ■

Finally, we can mention groups of people or individual contexts that have been known to have tried mentoring in one form or another, to illustrate the potential of mentoring to assist in various functions in many fields. The key feature of this list is its variety. Some of these applications bear very little relation or proximity to some of the others, yet all of them involve an element of mentoring.

- Graduate orientation to work

- Graduate induction

- Managers preparing for promotion

- Managers being induced into a new role

- Managers on structured learning programmes

- Affirmative action for disadvantaged groups – disabled, ethnic minorities, women

- Changes in job role

- Senior managers' peer mentoring

- Librarians continuing professional development

- Role modelling for young offenders

- Support for entrepreneurs in small businesses.

The role of process adviser or consultant
■ ■ ■

What does a mentor need to do to have fully covered the requirements of the context base?

1 Understand the context requirements

The mentor will need to feel confident with his/her own involvement and approach. Each individual context will bring with it a particular set of requirements. These are often quite explicit, particularly if there is a structured programme.They may be special requirements and outputs such as tests, qualifications, assignments, projects, and so on. The mentor will need to understand the criteria by which progress will be measured.

There may also be some kind of guide or guidance notes on the nature and objectives of the relationship. Mentors are likely to get to understand these by one or a combination of the following:

- A briefing

- Structured training

- Directed reading

- Discussion

- Guidance notes

- Manuals

Mentors will need to have access to someone who understands or 'owns' the context that surrounds this particular relationship. This will give them the opportunity to ask questions and confirm their own understanding of the requirements.

A major part of the mentor's function will be to check progress and to check that the learner is advancing according to the criteria that have been set. An additional check will be whether the learner understands and does the same checking review process for him/herself.

2 Help the learner to set objectives

This requirement will apply to any kind of context. In more open-frame or informal types of mentor–learner relationship there will be a low level of focus on the context base. Nonetheless, the learner will still be seeking to set personal objectives and will have to define outputs and manage his/her time in order to deliver them effectively.

In more formal and structured programmes the external requirements will mean that the learner will have to time-manage the process at a fairly detailed level. It is always useful to set targets. This is particularly true where the outputs are considerable. Encouraging learners to break major tasks down into 'mind-sized' chunks is a good discipline. This can be done by making objectives SMART.

S Specific
M Measurable
A Achievable
R Realistic
T Time-related.

3 Manage time

In the first instance, learners may not be good at managing their time. They may need help in prioritising tasks and setting realistic targets.

4 Interpret the requirements of the programme

Although the learners may have been briefed or supplied with substantial amounts of information at the early stages of the relationship, they may not have fully internalised this or interpreted its significance for them. This needs to be checked out and mentors may be able to move along this process.

5 Monitor progress

It is always the role of the mentor to ask searching questions about the amount of progress that has been made. Such questions might include:

- What tasks have you completed?
- What tasks have you not completed?

- How well have you completed them?
- How do you feel about the results?
- What went well?
- What was difficult?
- How did you go about it?
- What have you learnt?
- What next?

■ Skillcheck

Because much of the business of the context base is task-focused, the skills of the process adviser are those of any good manager who is used to allocating work, monitoring progress and developing people. Skills include:

- Setting objectives

- Planning tasks

- Project management.

'The idea is so simple, just getting two people together who can support each other. But the simplest ideas are often the best.'

Chapter 6

■ ■ ■

Helping people to learn

■ *Key learning points*

1 Learning for adults at work is different from the way many of us learnt at school.

2 Kolb's learning cycle – learning can be thought of as a four-stage cycle.

3 We have individual preferences which make up our own learning style. There are four basic learning styles.

4 How do we use our knowledge of the learning styles to promote and facilitate learning for others?

5 The major role models in this base are those of coach and learning consultant.

6 There is a repertoire of skills that equips mentors to facilitate learning in others.

For many of us our default notion of what constitutes learning is related to our school or early educational experience. For all too many of us that experience was negative. When adults are asked to recall their early experiences of education, these memories are dominated by words like:

- knowledge ■ books   ■ exams   ■ fear   ■ boredom
- memory   ■ teachers   ■ facts.

The model on which these notions are based seems to go as follows:

1 The teacher has the knowledge and the skill.

2 The teacher tells us what we need to know (supplemented by the acquisition of knowledge through reading books).

3 They teach what we need to be able to do – the acquisition of skills.

4 We practice (and get told off and labelled 'dumb' when we get it wrong).

5 We then take exams and tests to demonstrate how much we know (or how much we can remember of what we know).

This teacher-led approach is knowledge based. The teacher has the knowledge and the skill and has the responsibility of passing it on to us. It is dominated by right-answer seeking and is seen as being intolerant of mistakes. Of course, all schools and all school education is not like that, but it is surprising how this view of it dominates the thinking of many mature adults. Many people have unfortunately carried these negative connotations over into their adult lives.

It is interesting that this stereotypic notion ignores some very important facts. What it ignores is that we learn some of the most important and fundamental things in our lives very early on and without any tuition at all. For instance, we learn to walk without tuition. We learn the enormous complexities of language without exams. We learn to cooperate and socialise with other people without any lessons.

The sadness is that many schools were able to take accomplished learners (five-year-old children) and convince them that they were unable to master the simple arts of, for instance, addition and subtraction.

For many years, much adult education has been based on this simplistic, pedagogical model of how people learn. It is worth saying that education in schools has changed substantially since the 1960s, with the development of many more sophisticated ideas about how children learn.

Changes, too, have happened in the world of adult education. A number of basic challenges have faced those who are interested in fostering and encouraging learning for adults. One is how do we develop ideas, tools, techniques, habits and processes that are more appropriate and effective to learning in general? Another is how do we develop approaches that are more appropriate for adults, as opposed to children? Finally, how can we develop the transfer of learning from the classroom to work?

In Chapter 1 we looked at how the world of learning is changing in organisations. We are moving away from the course-led and instructor-led approaches to learning. Learning is becoming more learner-focused, not only in its delivery, but also in terms of ownership. That is to say that people at work are increasingly having to take more and more responsibility for their own learning. Added to this, more of this learning is taking place in the working environment, rather than in the classroom.

The role of the manager
■ ■ ■

As responsibility for learning and development has moved from the classroom and the human resources departments to the line and to the individuals themselves, so pressure has increased on managers to fulfil the role of developer.

Many good managers are naturally good developers of people. Inasmuch as they are, they are already good 'natural' mentors. However, many are not. So people who are willing to take responsibility for their own learning often need to find others to act as guides for their learning. This explains the growth in the interest and practice of mentoring.

We need to develop approaches to learning that are more sophisticated than the teacher-pupil, knowledge transfer model, and we need to be able to harness the formidable abilities of adults to drive their own learning.

Adults are sophisticated learners
■ ■ ■

We need to bear in mind that, as learners, adults have different needs from children. There are several assumptions that we should make about how we approach adults as learners. Among other factors, we should consider:

98

- Adults are already experienced and successful learners

- Adults need to take responsibility for their own learning

- Adults need to participate fully and equally in their own learning.

Learner confidence
■ ■ ■

However, we should not assume that learning is an easy option for adults. We have a good deal of evidence to show that it is not. Adults may well be fluent and confident in relation to certain specified areas, with which they are familiar, but may not be so confident outside those areas. For instance, for people in the finance function, it may be easy to graft on to their current knowledge or skill base some new ideas or techniques about the practice of financial management. However, when faced with a need to learn about strategy, say, or communication skills, they may be much less confident.

Generic learner confidence can be measured by reference to two simple criteria:

- The ability to set high but achievable goals

■ The ability to take responsibility for their own learning.

These, in turn, may be affected by previous education, experience or exposure to the areas in question. Clearly, if people score highly on these criteria, they will be confident learners, almost by definition. Where they cannot, they may be naive learners, with low learner confidence. Mentors need to take into account where someone may be on this learner confidence scale (Figure 6), because approaches to, or styles of, mentoring should be adjusted accordingly.

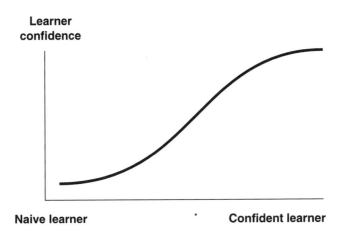

Fig 6   The learner confidence curve

A look at the curve and the criteria mentioned above will suggest that highly confident learners will need a fairly low level of direction. Naive learners, on the other hand, may be more dependent in their needs. They may need a higher level of direction from their mentors. In the early days of a relationship, it may be appropriate to satisfy this level of dependency. However, the sooner mentors can 'push' the learners up the confidence curve, the sooner the learners will be able to become more of self-starters for themselves. This should be an explicit aim of the relationship.

Mentors should also take into account how people go about learning. To do this, mentors will need to know about the learning cycle.

The Kolb learning cycle
■ ■ ■

One model of the learning process, which seems much more suitable for adults in working environments, is that developed by an American psychologist, David Kolb. He conceived of learning as being a cyclical process (Figure 7).

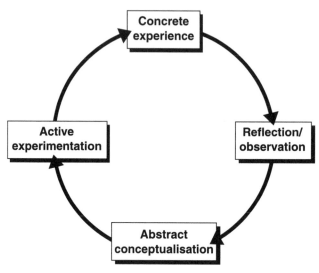

Fig 7   The Kolb learning cycle

Concrete experience

We are all engaged in an enormous variety of complex experiences during our working lives. Such experiences can be positive or negative, emotional or behavioural, and can happen in a planned or an accidental way. This is the 'sleeves rolled up' stage of the learning cycle.

Reflection or observation

Reflection is the process of taking stock of our experiences and the significance they hold for us. It happens when we begin to try to make sense of our own experience. It is a process of structured and thoughtful noticing and evaluating of the things that happen to us. It is perfectly natural, and an important component of learning. If you have ever had the experience of attending a training course and someone asks you what you learnt, it can happen that people say something along the line of: 'Oh, the course was not too good, but I learnt an awful lot in the bar in the evening.' This is an indication of how reflection can enable learning.

Abstract conceptualisation

This is the stage (also called theorising) where we build structures of explanations for the way the world works. We develop theories, or rules, to define our expectations and cause–effect chains.

The need for such a stage can be illustrated and verified by much of our own experience. Take the example of young people of school age who are given the 'rules', for instance, for the way that the world of numbers works. Yet it is known to be very difficult for people to remember and apply some of the very simple mechanical rules ('turn it upside down and multiply', 'borrow one and pay it back', 'a minus and a minus make a plus', and so on). Why is this? It is often because they have been unable to internalise the rules as sets of reasonable explanations for the way that the world of numbers works. They have, effectively, missed out on this stage, and that inhibits learning and the development of effective skills.

101

Active experimentation

This is the stage at which we test out our structures of explanations against the real world. Checking things out against reality enables us to verify our predictions and guesses against our experience. The resulting experience is fed back into the system and the loop begins again. This can be shown by a very simple game analogy.

Experience	– We watch people playing a new game.
Reflection / observation	– We note what happens and who does what.
Conceptualisation	– We work out the rules and aims of the game.
Experimentation	– We play the game.

You may also be able to identify where the learning cycle fits much more naturally with natural learning events such as learning to ride a bicycle or play an instrument.

The model has proved quite robust when applied to the way that adults seem to learn work-related skills and behaviours. It seems to have a high face validity – in other words, it seems to ring true of people's experiences of learning.

Using the learning cycle
■ ■ ■

If we want to promote learning and to maximise opportunities for learning from work-based activities and situations, then the learning cycle, coupled with some basic skills, is a simple yet powerful starting point. There are questions, challenges and checks that can be made at each stage of any activity, to review progress and to move people around the learning cycle, so that they can capture as much of the learning opportunity that experience affords.

Here are some examples, and ideas, but it is fairly easy to develop your own.

Experience

In this stage of the learning cycle, what the mentor can do is to help to *structure* experience. This can be done by planning and organising, and may involve using tools and techniques. But, as with all of the other mentor interventions, one of the most powerful forms of intervention is the judicious use of questions.

- What are you going to do?

- How are you going to go about it?

- Why are you hesitating?

- Do you feel ready/confident?

Reflection

At this stage of the learning cycle, the mentor can act as a *focuser* on experience. In other words, what the mentor can do is to encourage the learner to pay explicit attention to previous experience and to explore and review the significance of that experience.

- How did it go?

- What went wrong?

- What went right?

- How did it feel?

Conceptualisation

At this stage, learners should be encouraged to begin to make sense of their experiences, and to make connections with other experiences and known bodies of knowledge. Learners should be *modelling experience*, generalising, trying to understand cause-and-effect processes and other patterns.

- Do you know what is happening?

- Why does that work in that way?

- What models/techniques are you using?

- What is the process?

Experimenting

This is the *reality check* stage. Learners should be trying to gauge if and how things will work in practice. Are their ideas and predictions realistic?

- Will it work?

- How is that of use?

Such simple questioning processes can have a number of beneficial effects:

- They can move people around the learning cycle

- They can help to develop self-awareness

- They can help to capture the learning potential of any situation.

Learning styles
■ ■ ■

Work by D. Honey and A. Mumford* identified that we are not equally skilled or comfortable at each of the four stages of the learning cycle. Most of us have preferences in relation to these stages. We should bear in mind that for most people these preferences are not exclusive. That is, we have strengths and weaknesses, but very few of us are unable to operate at all at any of these stages. These strengths and weaknesses can be described by one of the four basic learning styles. Honey and Mumford classified these four basic styles, based on the stages of the Kolb learning cycle.

Activist

These people are comfortable operating at the experience stage of the learning cycle. Activists enjoy getting involved in new experiences. They seek out new opportunities, take on problems and challenges. They tend to be comfortable in the limelight, and often adopt high-profile activities, such as chairing meetings, leading discussions, giving presentations, and so on.

Activists learn best when:

- They can immerse themselves in here-and-now activities

- There is an element of adrenaline or risk

- They can 'spark' off other people.

They are less likely to learn when:

- They have to take a passive role

- They have to assimilate large amounts of data

- They are engaged in solitary activities.

* *A Manual of Learning Styles*, P. Honey Publications, 1982, Maidenhead

Reflectors

Reflectors like to take time, to think things through from various angles before acting. They are cautious and measured, preferring to collect information to mull over before reaching conclusions. They prefer to listen and watch, rather than involve themselves too much. They would normally tend to be of a lower profile than the activists.

They learn best when:

- They are given time to think things over
- They have access to all of the information
- Decisions or actions are not needed in a rush.

They learn least when:

- They are rushed or pressurised

105

- They don't have the relevant data
- They are forced to adopt a high profile.

Theorists

Theorists assimilate, integrate and synthesise information about the world into rational schemes, structures or theories, or systems of explanation. They are interested in principles, assumptions, objectivity and logic. They will seek to fit new experiences into their own scheme of things. They may react against superficiality and subjectivity.

They learn best when:

- They can use systems or models of the world that make sense to them
- They have a chance to explore connectivity and relationships between facts and ideas
- Subject matter is objective and based on rational principles.

They learn least when:

- They are 'dropped in at the deep end'

- They don't know the rationale for what they are doing

- Emotions or feelings are involved.

Pragmatists

Pragmatists value new ideas, not as an end in themselves, but to see if they work in practice. They are down to earth and enjoy getting on with practical activities and problem-solving. They may be impatient with theoretical or open-ended discussion, preferring to get on with things. A strong consideration will be 'How does that work?' or 'What use is that?'.

They learn best when:

- They can see a link to real-world applications

- They can try things out – preferably without too much delay

- They can deal with practical issues.

They learn least when:

- They can't relate the matter in hand to the real world

- There is too much theory

- The practical benefit isn't obvious.

Of course, it is worth saying that people can be relatively balanced in relation to these four styles. Experience shows that most people easily recognise elements of their own characteristic behaviour from descriptions like those given above.

Using learning styles

■ ■ ■

How do learning styles affect the mentor–learner relationship?

One aim for the mentor is to create the right environment in which people can undertake these processes to complete the learning cycle and learn effectively. This has to be done while taking account of the fact that the learner will have a bias to one or more of the stages in the total process. Equally, there will be stages in the process that they typically ignore.

The preferences of both the mentor and the learner should be given consideration in the course of the relationship. This is a question of mutual self-knowledge and self-awareness. As the learning style relates to the way that people learn, the more we can know about ourselves and our own behaviour, the better.

One of the great benefits of such self-awareness is that it legitimates our own experiences and approaches. Thus, for instance, for stereotypical reflectors, it may reinforce their own self-confidence to know that they are very good and efficient at learning in their own style.

It will be important for a mentor to respect the favoured style of the learner. Having said that, a mentor can suggest or encourage new behaviours in the learner. For our stereotypical reflectors, once confidence has been gained, it is worth trying to help them to widen their own repertoire of skills and behaviours by encouraging them to:

107

- Have a go, or give it a try

- Build their thoughts into a coherent pattern or explanation

- Check if their idea is practical.

A similar thing would be true for anyone who had strong preferences or weaknesses in relation to any of the learning styles.

Mentor-learner pairings
■ ■ ■

Two issues to be addressed, for both the mentor and the learner, are those of how to develop the relationship and how the relationship is affected when the styles of the mentor and the learner are different. Much of this, as always, is about mutual self-knowledge and mutual respect.

For a strongly activist mentor, it could possibly be frustrating working with a highly reflective learner. He/she may well have a tendency to 'push things on' too quickly when the learner isn't ready.

Similarly, what happens if both the learner and the mentor have the same learning style? There are some dangers here.

The advantage is that the pairing may find it easier to gain rapport as their approaches may be similar. However, the disadvantage could be that the learner may feel that his/her own approach is not being sufficiently respected and valued.

Where there is a difference in learning styles, the mentor may have things to learn from the approach of the learner. However, there is a potential benefit for the learner, in that he/she can gauge the approach of the mentor and can possibly develop and widen his/her own repertoire of behaviours by watching and listening.

108

These changes are among the most powerful potential benefits of the mentor–learner relationship. However, it can only happen if:

- They both have an understanding of their own learning styles

- They share knowledge and awareness with each other.

It is important for mentors to find out about their own learning styles and those of their learners. There are numerous ways to do this.

There is a self-test which can be used to give a profile or inventory of individual learning styles. If this is impractical for any reason, then the mentor could make a judgement based on the descriptions given above.

Now you can give some thought as to how you might mentor someone with strong preferences in each of the learning styles.

- What questions do you need to ask?

- What are you likely to be able to offer them?

- What are likely to be the differences?

Role models

■　■　■

The two basic roles associated with the development base of mentoring are the learning consultant and coach.

The learning consultant

There are many processes and activities that mentors can be involved with that will enhance and facilitate learning for others. Mostly, they will do this by focusing explicitly on the learning processes, needs and outcomes for the learner.

They will focus on learning needs by asking questions and by helping the learners to audit their own strengths and weaknesses. They will focus on the learning process by asking the learners how they intend to go about things, by setting goals, and so on. Reference back to the 'Using the learning cycle' section will show how to relate activities and experience to the learning cycle.

The coach

Coaching is probably the key skill within the development base of mentoring and it needs some consideration in its own right. What is coaching? Coaching is a process of assisting in the transfer of skill or competence to another person. It involves guiding someone through a set of experiences with the aim of improving or developing performance.

But what makes coaching different from 'teaching'? Teaching involves showing someone how to do something. We either perform the task or instruct someone on how to perform it. This can be a useful and productive way for someone to learn. However, it is not as powerful as coaching. The idea of coaching comes from the sporting arena. With coaching, we do not show or tell people how to do something. What we do is to surround their activity with a set of processes that enables them to learn from the situation. These processes include asking questions, checking feelings, focusing on the details of a situation. Coaching is much more about asking than telling. An instruction to:

> 'Make sure you have that plan prepared ...'

has a number of disadvantages. First, instructions are never interpreted in the same positive and supportive way as questions. Secondly, the instruction tells them what to do, but it gives no indication as to how to do it. It does not take account of prevailing circumstances, the situation or the individual. Instructions don't enable a learner to focus on what is happening or how it is happening.

Some skills involve physical processes. As such, in order to improve performance, people need to pay attention to sensory information in order to improve. Many higher level work-based skills involve the mastery of more abstract or analytical processes. In order to be competent, people need 'process efficiency'. To improve, they have to pay attention to process, and questions that focus attention on the way we do things are the best way to do this.

We get it by paying attention to:

- Planning
- Self-awareness
- Attitude and confidence
- Monitoring
- Adjusting to circumstances
- Thinking about results.

In terms of performance, there are three key areas that we need to pay attention to.

This combination of those things we know and understand, those that we feel, and those that we can do, add up to a complete description of our capability.

Knowledge ◄──► Attitude ◄──► Skill

The 3-dimensional approach to coaching
■ ■ ■

The coaching intervention can be thought of as a three-stage process known as the 3D approach: Define, Describe, Decide.

Step 1: Define

At the initial stage we need to identify some goals. We need to answer the question: *What do you want?*

The way to go about this is to ask people questions that narrow them down to specific goals. People may approach the broad question with quite a broad answer – an aim. That is perfectly appropriate, but they also need guiding to some specific goal – a SMART goal.

■ CASE STUDY

A coaching conversation

Alan comes along to a mentoring session and presents a problem. He is dissatisfied with his ability to write written reports and proposals. An initial conversation might go something like this:

'I'm not very happy about my written reports.'

'In what way?'

'Well, first, they aren't very good, and second, I find them really difficult to write.'

'So what would you like instead?'

'Well, the opposite.'

'Can you be more specific?'

'Well, Terry, my director, criticises my monthly marketing report. I would like it to pass the "Terry test" for once.'

'OK. When is the next one due?'

'In three weeks time.'

'And what do you think we can get out of today's session?'

'Well, I'd like to get a good idea of what is wrong, and I would like to have some kind of plan or structure to work on for the next report.'

Notice the combination of open questions ('In what way?'), and closed questions ('When is the next one due?'). This enables the coach to elicit quality information, while closing in on a SMART goal. As so often in these situations, the goals operate on a number of levels – the broader, long-term goal, and the specific goal for this one session.

In this way, at Step 1 we have the problem defined and the goal specified.

Step 2: Describe

At the next stage we are trying to 'put the flesh on the bones' of the problem or situation. This is the reality-check stage. It answers the question: *what's happening?*

The keys to this stage are the awareness of the learner and the amount of detail that can be found. In terms of most working contexts, it might involve:

- Facts

- Figures

- Incidents

- Processes

- Attitudes, etc.

There are two places where such information can come from:

- **From the individual concerned.** The learner may know what is wrong. It is always worth checking if his/her descriptions are accurate. Notice that we use the word description, not judgement. Expressions like 'It's just useless' may or may not be true, but they give no detail and only serve to demotivate.

- **From feedback.** In the case of our writer, the feedback may have come from his director, or it may come from us, if we examine an example of the writing.

At this stage, it will be useful to give some guidelines for giving feedback.

1 Focus on behaviour not on the person.

2 Focus on observation rather than on inference, intuition or guesses.

3 Focus on description rather than judgement.

4 Focus on the specific rather than the general.

5 Balance the negative with the positive.

If good feedback focuses on information rather than judgement, then people are in a position to know what changes need to be made. One of the main purposes of the 'Describe' phase is to get people to notice – to achieve awareness. This is often half the battle. The adjustment then becomes much easier.

For our writer, it soon becomes clear to him that the writing is too unstructured and waffles too far from the subject. It also emerges from his description of how he goes about writing that the nature of the output is related to the way he writes, which is why it is so difficult. Basically, he writes at a single sitting and just 'dumps' all of his thoughts more or less as they come to his mind.

Step 3: Decide

This is the stage where options are generated and evaluated. It answers the question: *what are you going to do about it?*

If the Description stage is done properly and fully, then the options are usually obvious. It is better if the learner gets the chance to put up his/her own suggestions, although the coach/mentor should make appropriate suggestions. Although the options may be obvious, there is always the attitude/confidence issue to take into account.

In the case of our writer, he had himself identified the need to plan and structure his documents. The coach/mentor was able to suggest a new technique – mind mapping. Invited to use this plan to write the next marketing report, a great improvement was effected. This, again, was consolidated by the asking of questions:

113

- Is that OK?

- How is the structure?

- How do you feel now?

- Does this work as the plan you needed?

To summarise, then, the processes involved are:

- Defining an aim

- Checking out the current situation – What is the problem?

- Defining some objectives or targets for improvement

- Planning some experiences

- Monitoring – How are they doing? How do they feel?

- Giving feedback where appropriate

- Re-adjusting.

It is a continuous loop that involves knowledge and attitude as well as skill. It is not so different from the plan–action–review cycle known so well by managers. Where it differs is that it encompasses the whole person and that the monitoring and feedback are done continuously and in real-time if possible. The whole process is driven by the asking of questions that enable the learners to be aware of, and work with, their own experiences.

Good managers are natural coaches

■ ■ ■

When we look at the naturally occurring types of intervention that involve learning, coaching is rated as second only to mentoring itself. It is highly valued by those who are the recipients of the coaching. Coaching is a natural and necessary component of management. There is some evidence that managers who are seen as effective are those who are good at coaching.

Other issues that affect learning activities

■ ■ ■

We have set out in an ordered way the kinds of role and the kinds of intervention that assist people in learning at work. However, we must never forget that learning is a hit-and-miss process. Those who are involved in it are real people – and they bring with them all of the hopes and fears that you would expect. Learning is not a simple, scientific and objective business, and this needs to be acknowledged and taken into account by mentors. When dealing with real people, we should take into account:

- Confidence
- Level of challenge
- Perceived appropriateness
- Demands of the job.

■ *Skillcheck*

As learning is one of the key areas of activity for the mentor–learner relationship, the skill requirements are quite comprehensive. In all of the discussion above, a number of skills keep recurring, and that is a testimony to their importance. They are based around the key roles of coach and learning consultant.

Skills required to promote learning:

- Coaching

- Setting goals

- Giving feedback

- Questioning

- Listening

- Challenging

- Modelling

- Supporting

- Structuring experience

- Monitoring.

The key qualities relating to the development base of mentoring are:

- **Developmental orientation.** This involves a desire to see other people develop. Mentors provide the wherewithal to help and guide people through that development process. The qualities include patience and perceptiveness.

- **Empowering orientation.** People who have this quality give scope to other people to act on their own initiative. They tend to delegate effectively and are not afraid to release authority. Qualities include self-confidence.

'On one level I think
mentoring is really trying to
bring back some of the best
elements of the extended
family, but in a more
formal way.'

Chapter 7

■ ■ ■

Mentoring relationships

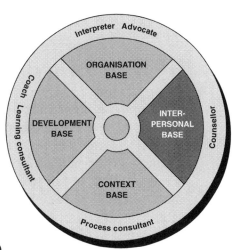

■ *Key learning points*

1   The interpersonal base is the anchor for the whole mentoring relationship.

2   There are certain core conditions that need to be present to make any relationship productive.

3   The key role model for the mentor is that of counsellor.

4   We look at the skills and processes involved in the counselling part of the role.

In this chapter we focus on the nature of the relationship between the mentor and the learner. The interpersonal (or relationship) base is probably the most important for both the mentor and the learner. This is because it is, in a sense, the 'anchor' of the whole mentor–learner process. If the relationship is not productive and comfortable on an interpersonal basis, then the rest will not follow. It is important at the outset to establish a relationship that is both professional and meaningful. If either party is uncomfortable, the basic purposes of the mentor–learner relationship will not be satisfied. This makes it sound critical, and indeed it is, but there is no need to feel daunted. There are a few mitigating considerations.

The first is that most of us have a good level of generic communication skills, and the ability to develop productive relationships quite naturally. For most mentors, this is likely to be second nature. Secondly, there is no 'identikit' picture that defines how this relationship is conducted. Personal style and a natural approach are perfectly in order.

But where we are entering into relationships with a purpose, we need to think about the key questions, which are:

- What form should this relationship take?

- How does it develop?

- What are the key skills required?

The interpersonal frame

■ ■ ■

Let us look first at the components of any good, effective working relationship. Such relationships tend to be characterised by three components. As mentoring is a term taken from the Greeks, perhaps it is appropriate that this is defined by three terms known well to the Greeks.

- Ethos

- Pathos

- Logos.

Ethos

This describes the moral dimension of the relationship. It is about saying what you mean, and meaning what you say. A good ethos comes with consistency of message. Whether we are delivering good or difficult messages, there is an element of integrity and honesty about the message. Key words here are:

- Congruence

- Integrity

- Trust

- Honesty

- Sincerity

- Credibility

- Values.

121

Relationships develop their own style and character, and these can be good, bad or indifferent. It is possible to develop relationships in a climate of mistrust and suspicion, where posturing is more important than substance and where seniority is a critical dimension. However, such relationships tend not to be productive.

On the other hand, effective relationships tend to be characterised by the words listed above. In such relationships people feel free to be honest and are not always on their guard. There is invariably a sense of substance and common purpose in these relationships.

How do we display ethos? Genuine concern for, and interest in, the other person and for the substance of his/her conversations is a good way of developing ethos. But perhaps a simpler way to describe this is to say that if you are not genuine, and your exchanges do not have integrity from your point of view, the learner will pick up this from the verbal and non-verbal elements of your behaviour.

Pathos

Pathos describes a genuine interest in the other person as a person in his/her own right. It is the 'hearts' of the 'hearts and minds' aspect of the relationship. It is where we appeal to and engage that other person at a real emotional level. It is also a recognition of what the other person brings to the relationship, that is, all of those things that makes the person human – emotions, hopes, fears, ambitions, and so on.

The key words here are:

- Empathy

- Warmth

- Positive regard

- Disclosure

- Rapport.

We establish pathos by dealing directly with these things. How do learners feel about what they are doing, and what they are about to do? What do they want to achieve? What bothers them? What excites them? If we can genuinely share emotions, both positive and negative, and acknowledge the interests and concerns of others, we are developing pathos.

Think about most one-to-one meetings with people whom you don't know too well. The conversation usually starts with a few simple 'ice-breakers'. Questions such as 'how was the journey?', 'how are you?', etc., are a simple recognition of the importance of the human dimension. They may sound trivial, but they are steps towards acknowledging and engaging in the pathos or human dimension of the interaction.

As well as seeking to engage other people at this level, we have to give a little of ourselves. So, as well as acknowledging and recognising, we should quite naturally disclose something about our own experiences, feelings and emotions. When we do this we achieve rapport. This is a state of being comfortable and 'in tune' with the other person.

The ethos and pathos together comprise what we might call the *social agenda* of interpersonal interactions. We make a mistake if we think of conversations, even at work, as being just about plans, budgets, competencies or whatever. A great deal of the agenda of any interpersonal interaction is the unspoken agenda of two people making connections. This is why we prefer some people, we enjoy some conversations, more than others – we feel more or less comfortable. Furthermore, a great deal of this is not about the substantive content of the conversation itself.

Particularly in the early part of a relationship, we need to pay attention to this unspoken but vital part of the relationship. It is what makes it not only enjoyable, but also productive.

Logos

Logos is the logical and objective element of the relationship. It is the substantive content of the conversations – the goals, techniques, outcomes and so on, of the conversations. It is difficult to be specific about this aspect of the interpersonal frame because it is as varied and as wide as the substance of the conversations between two people over an extended period of time. In general, though, it is just whatever the two people choose to talk about.

123

In most descriptions of relationships and communication between two individuals, it is this third component which we focus on. Yet this threefold description is useful precisely because it reinforces that the explicit content is not the only issue in communication. It is all too easy for people to forget to pay attention to the more implicit or intangible components of relationships. Yet they are equally as important. In fact, it is not exaggerating to say that you rarely get to grips fully or effectively with the substantive content if you haven't invested time and effort in establishing the ethos and pathos first.

The nature of one-to-one relationships
■ ■ ■

We tend to make the assumption that communication between two people is all about the words that are spoken. Research has identified that, in fact, words account for only a small proportion of the information that passes between two people in a one-to-one conversation. What accounts for the rest? Figure 8 illustrates the other elements.

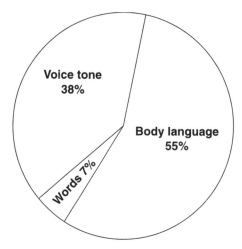

Fig 8 The elements of communication

Words

It is usually easy to know what the words part is all about. It is where we focus nearly all of our conscious attention. It may be surprising or even shocking that it represents only about 7 per cent of the information that passes in a one-to-one conversation.

Body language

Most people now accept that we give and receive a substantial amount of information non-verbally when we communicate. This information is communicated by the following:

- Body posture
- Gestures
- Eyes
- Facial expression
- Breathing patterns
- Skin tone.

We certainly 'read' this information, although most of it is received below the level of consciousness. As the information itself is non-verbal, so we tend to interpret or understand it non-verbally. This can cause problems when it comes to trying to interpret this kind of information in a purely verbal or rational way. There are books that purport to be a lexicography of non-verbal behaviour. That is, they claim to be able to 'translate' particular non-verbal gestures into words. The problem here is that meanings may not only be non-verbal, they are also highly individual.

Some gross or overt non-verbal behaviours are fairly easy to interpret. Extreme agitation, discomfort, sadness or distress can often be spotted. But for smaller scale and less obvious elements of non-verbal behaviour, their 'interpretation' should be checked back with the other person. As we get to know someone, we are often able to identify what certain postures, gestures, expressions and other habits mean.

Voice tone

Whereas many people understand something about the importance of body language, the information that is represented by voice tone is rarely considered or discussed. Yet a substantial amount of communication is in the voice tone, which suggests that we are quite sensitive to it. Equally, we are fairly untutored in its use. The information comes in terms of:

- Volume
- Pitch
- Rhythm
- Tone
- Speed.

That we are sensitive to the voice can be demonstrated by a few simple experiments.

Example 1. Think of how a mother uses her voice to influence the mood of a young baby. What happens to the voice?

Example 2. Think of a telephone conversation you have had with an unknown person, where you have formed a good or positive impression of that person. What was it about the voice that affected you? Also think of a time where you formed a negative impression. What qualities of the voice put you off? Did the voice enable you to visualise the person at the other end?

If it is difficult to interpret non-verbal behaviour, then how can we use non-verbal behaviour to enhance our communicative effectiveness? The answer is in two parts: first, we have to notice; second, we have to feed back.

Noticing

Trying to 'read' non-verbal behaviour consciously is very hard work. We have to train ourselves to notice what is going on. It is difficult because it is a counter-intuitive thing to do, but it is also difficult because to focus on the non-verbal behaviour means that we will probably lose the information contained in the words. Effective communicators are able to 'toggle' between verbal and non-verbal information. As an exercise, it is worth trying to watch and listen for five minutes a day to those things that you don't normally pay attention to. You will be surprised what you see and hear.

Feeding back

There are many books that go into enormous detail about non-verbal techniques of communication, such as mirroring, matching, and so on. We don't have space here to go into such depth, even if it were appropriate to do so. However, information flows in both directions, and we know that people adjust mutually to each other's non-verbal behaviour. That is, I have a natural tendency to respond to your signals, and you have a natural tendency to respond to mine. Good communicators are fluent in terms of acknowledging and giving back non-verbally some of the important information that they receive. They seem to be able to adjust their behaviour in the direction of that of the other person. The good news is that this 'follow my leader' feedback dance is perfectly natural and is what happens when people get 'in tune' with each other. This is what rapport is.

However, we don't want to suggest that only the non-verbal component of behaviour is important. Words may only account for 7 per cent of the information, but they are a critical 7 per cent. The importance of *listening* should not be underestimated. The words that people use give clues to the concepts and criteria important to them, and this can only be explored by listening.

But what do good listeners do? Again, this is a question of feedback. Good listeners use a repertoire of non-verbal and minimal verbal cues to keep the other person talking. Good listeners use phrases such as:

'yes'
'I understand'
'and what then?'
'uhum'.

These all serve to keep a conversation going.

Good listeners also tend to do a lot of the following:

127

1 *Use the 66:33 rule.* That is, they tend to listen at least 66 per cent of the time and talk a maximum of 33 per cent of the time.

2 *Acknowledge.* They give verbal recognition that they have heard what the talker has said.

3 *Show interest.* Although there is a verbal component to this, they tend to use non-verbal means to show they are engaged.

4 *Ask more than they tell.* They use open questions to gain information without specifying the answer and closed questions to check detail.

5 *Summarise.* This is the feedback. It says, in effect, *'this is what I understand you are saying – is it correct?'*

Counselling
■ ■ ■

In the interpersonal base of the mentoring wheel the major role models are those of friend/confidante and counsellor. The word 'counselling' itself can sometimes be a barrier, as some people regard it as a 'soft' option that somehow involves dabbling in a quasi-therapeutic area where they don't feel qualified. These reservations are unjustified, as counselling is a fairly common-sense process that has a lot of uses and many potential benefits in the management context.

Of course, there are many definitions of counselling, most of which reflect the interests or priorities of the person doing the defining. In a working context, a good definition is:

> Counselling is a way of responding and relating to people so that they feel clearer about what is concerning them. They then feel bet-ter able to help themselves and make their own decisions. It helps them to talk about and work out what their feelings are, before taking any action. It is this exploration and understanding, before action, which is special about counselling.
> [In summary] counselling is about helping people to help them-selves.

(*Motivating for Change*, Nicola Phillips, Pitman, 1995)

Because of the sensitive and highly personal nature of such con-versations, it is important that they take place 'off-line'. Although good managers can, and do, counsel, it is important for a mentor, whether he/she is the line manager of the learner or not, to consider the conversation as separate and distinct from normal line management activities.

When to counsel
■ ■ ■

There are a number of issues to be tackled here. What distin-guishes counselling from everyday one-to-one conversation or communication is not the set of skills required, but the situation. Experienced mentors (and experienced managers) know when to switch into counselling mode. What are the typical characteris-tics of these situations?

1 They tend not to be primarily about operational matters, although they may incorporate them or refer to them.

2 They tend not to be primarily about performance issues or

competence – these are more likely to be situations for a coaching input.

3 They tend to involve problems, difficulties, blockages, frustrations, relationship difficulties. In addition, there is usually some unknown dimension – why things are happening the way they are, or what to do about it.

4 They involve the individual at a deep personal level. This may include emotions, hopes, fears, values and so on. There may well be some negative impact on the individual – from discomfort to outright distress.

Here are some typical examples:

A supervisor at work has to write a report. On investigation, it emerges that the supervisor has not written a formal document for over twenty years. Not surprisingly, he/she is lacking confidence in his/her own ability.

129

A junior female executive is frustrated because her manager won't delegate sufficiently challenging work. She sees this as a block in her progress. When she tries to talk to her manager, to request some work that will challenge her more, she is blocked.

A senior manager has undergone a 360 degree appraisal. He has been confronted with some elements of his own behaviour as others see him. Their perception of his behaviour is quite at odds with his own. He has been confronted with the facts that he is very tough-minded, does not listen and makes decisions without taking into account the opinions or interests of other people.

The 3-dimensional approach to counselling
■ ■ ■

Good counselling approaches seem to agree that counselling conversations have three basic steps. We shall call them:

1 Define

2 Describe

3 Decide.

Notice that the process is similar to that of coaching. However, the intervention and the way the process is applied is different.

Step 1: Define

The first stage involves setting outcomes. Counselling is a structured intervention, and is about more than the opportunity to talk or let off steam. This structure is initiated right at the beginning. Although the presenting problem is a starting point, it should be challenged. The key question is: *What do you want to get out of this?*

The more specific the answer, the better. One reason for challenging is that people often, as you would expect, present negative problems:

'I don't get on with people at work.'

If we offer the challenge,

'How would you like it to be?'

this pushes the individual to a positive statement. If they then respond,

'I would like to get on better with people at work.'

you have made some considerable progress. The statement has moved from negative to positive. It has moved from being a dissatisfaction to being a goal or an agenda. The new statement provides structure and purpose to the conversation.

Even this can be refined one stage further. A statement like,

'I want to feel better at work.'

is positive, but it does not indicate what 'better' would mean. The challenge here is to make it behaviourally specific.

'What would make you feel better at work?'

Step 2: Describe

Thereafter, stage two is about exploring the situation. To do this we need to allow the learner to talk. We need to use open questions and to remember to check for feelings and emotions as well as facts. In fact, we use all of the skills that were set out in the listening section above. This involves listening, acknowledging, checking, challenging and summarising, as we move from the general to the specific.

The basic objective here, for the mentor and the learner, is to understand and be aware of the basic dimensions of the problem.

It should be remembered that there are always some limitations to understanding the behaviour of another person. These potential 'blank' areas of a lack of understanding and awareness are described in the jo-hari window, which maps knowledge about the behaviour and intentions of an individual in two dimensions. The first dimension is that of the self-awareness of the individual. An individual may have a higher or lower awareness. The second dimension is how much the person reveals or discloses of him/herself to others. These are shown in Figure 9.

131

	Known to self	Not known to self
Known to others	OPEN	BLIND
Not known to others	HIDDEN	UNKNOWN

Fig 9   The jo-hari window

A mentor or counsellor can make judgements, based on behaviour and other information, as to the relative extents of the areas in the window. The information provided can then be used to determine an approach to suit the individual involved. This usually means developing either the mentor's awareness of the learner, or the learner's awareness of him/herself. It might also be used to gauge the accuracy and comprehensiveness of the understanding achieved in the second stage of counselling.

Step 3: Decide

The final phase involves the developing of solutions to the problem or issue at hand. The key here is to allow the learner to develop his/her own solution to the problem and one which suits his/her own learning needs and style. The temptation is always going to be for the mentor/counsellor to jump in and offer, or even impose, his/her own favoured solution to the problem. The real skill lies in being able to wait and to accept. The other skills involve challenging suggested solutions for their appropriateness and feasibility.

This stage is also about resourcing the agreed solutions to the problem. In this context, resourcing may mean solely supporting people through the process. But it might also mean finding resources in a more tangible sense.

As in other processes and at other stages, SMART goals are appropriate and useful here.

Counselling style

■ ■ ■

It is generally accepted that for problem-solving in the personal dimension the less interventionist approaches are more appropriate. The same is also true in a mentoring context. Part of the job description for the mentor that we set out in Chapter 2 was that the mentor supported the learner in the management of his/her own development. We have also suggested it should be explicitly part of the objectives that the learner take responsibility for his/her own learning, and by implication, the ownership of the solution to his/her own problems.

Learners are not going to be able to take full responsibility if the mentor, in his/her role as counsellor, insists on making all the running and inventing the solution to every problem. People will develop their own solutions to problems if the mentor gives them space to do so. This may involve some skills that are unfamiliar or new to the potential mentor.

For instance, very few of us have mastered the skill of managing silence. A natural inclination is to fill a space by inventing something to say. In a counselling context, a mentor should resist the temptation to fill all the spaces for the learner. Often the silence is valuable precisely because people are thinking deeply. Sometimes the most important things that people say are after a lengthy silence.

However, a mentor's individual style will reflect his/her own communication style and personal approaches. It may have elements of any or all of the following:

- **Evaluative** – based on judgement

- **Interpretative** – based on analysis

- **Supportive** – based on reassurance

- **Probing** – based on tough questioning

- **Understanding** – based on thoughts and feelings.

As mentors, we also need to feel comfortable with our approach. It is always worth checking with a learner if he/she values and appreciates our approach.

133

Letting go
■ ■ ■

As a final word about counselling, we should always remember that we are dealing with people in highly sensitive areas. People bring their innermost selves with them and they have a lot invested in the conversations and issues that they share with us. They disclose their feelings, hopes, fears and anxieties, they feel nervous. Also, the nature of the relationship usually involves change. This can mean a change of circumstances, but it more usually means a change of behaviour. It can be threatening. People have a strong desire to hold on to behaviour which has served them well, and in which they have developed a level of comfort. Thus, changing can challenge people's sense of self, as well as their habits. These changes, therefore, are not trivial for people. They can run very deep.

As mentors, we need to be aware of, and respect the implications of this. We need to recognise why it might be difficult to change and to anticipate and be sympathetic to the barriers that people face. We also need to keep an eye out for those situations where we ourselves feel out of our depth. A mentor should never be afraid to ask for advice and should be prepared to deal sensibly with situations that might need professional help or intervention.

■ *Skillcheck*

The list of key skills in the interpersonal base of the mentoring wheel is wide and comprehensive. However, for most of us, they come fairly naturally. It tends not to be the case that we either have them or don't have them. The question is to what extent do we have them?

The key skills involved are:

- Listening

- Questioning

- Self-evaluation

- Motivating

- Giving feedback

- Setting goals

- Creative problem-solving.

The key qualities are:

- **Accessibility.** Do you have the time and attention to devote to learners' needs?

- **Communication.** Can you make and maintain good relationships?

- **Inventiveness.** Are you open to new ideas and new ways of doing things? Are you a good problem-solver?

There is a whole set of qualities that we associate with good interpersonal communication, in the context of the interpersonal frame. These include:

- Empathy

- Trust

- Sincerity

- Emotional confidence

- Honesty.

'If you want to see improvement not just in the skills of individuals, but also to your business – get involved.'

Chapter 8

■ ■ ■

The mentoring manager

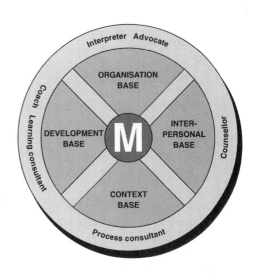

■ Key learning points

1 A mentoring relationship has a life cycle.

2 The terms of reference and broad agenda of the mentoring relationship should be agreed.

3 There are a set of tasks, based on the mentoring wheel, that need to be addressed.

4 A structured problem-solving or management process should be used to drive the agenda.

■ CASE STUDY

John Richards, Employment Department
(in *Management Matters*, Sept., 95)

'It does take time to do mentoring properly. But if the time is planned, it need not be onerous or interfere with the day-to-day running of the business. I would suggest to other mentors that, wherever possible, they put some time aside each week. This may not always be necessary, but it is easier to cancel a session than to try to find half an hour in a busy schedule.

The department got out of it two employees who have demonstrated their competence to an outside body. They are better prepared for the many, varying posts that can be found at their level and the levels above.

I got out of it involvement in the NVQ process and a better understanding of what NVQs and accrediting prior learning is all about. I also got a great deal of satisfaction when the evidence was completed and sent off.

Would I do it again? I already am. Another member of my team is following the same path and once again I have been asked to be a mentor to him. If you want to see improvement, not just in the skills of individuals but also to your business, get involved.'

We have now explored the details of the roles and primary tasks of each of the bases of the mentoring wheel. In this chapter we look at the M at the centre of the wheel. It is about the conduct of the mentor–learner relationship as a totality. At the centre of the wheel is where the four bases integrate and interweave. The four distinct bases don't operate in isolation, and the mentor-learner relationship has an integrated set of tasks and processes that bring them all together.

In this chapter we will look at some of the tasks and processes that need to take place in an effective mentoring relationship. Probably the easiest way to look at the development and flow of the relationship is in terms of a life cycle. A mentoring relationship has a life cycle of its own.

We can think of a mentor–learner relationship as having three phases:

- Phase I – Initiation
- Phase II – Growth and performance
- Phase III – Maturity.

Phase I: Initiation
■ ■ ■

Initiating and establishing a good relationship is the first and most important step. There are certain issues that need to be dealt with fairly early on. They are:

- Establishing rapport and trust
- Terms of reference
- Setting objectives.

139

Establishing rapport and trust

The relationship itself is the most important thing – even before you can 'get down to business'. In the interpersonal base we set out the concept of the social function of interpersonal communication. It is important to break the ice and establish the ethos and pathos before any productive work can be done. In the first instance, both you, as mentor, and the learner are likely to be nervous and unsure. The first aim is to begin to get comfortable with each other. Without this, none of the rest will follow.

Early discussions might involve:

- Getting to know each other as people
- Sharing a mutual understanding of roles.

Terms of reference

Terms of reference is another issue that should be discussed early on. This can sound rather formal or legalistic, but it doesn't have to be considered in that way. It may be more comfortable to think of it as an agreement about certain aspects of the relationship. In natural or more informal relationships it may hardly be discussed, although it will be agreed in an informal way.

At whatever level of formality you choose to deal with this, it is necessary to establish agreement on some quite basic dimensions of the relationship. Here are a few of the main dimensions that need to be considered.

Confidentiality

There needs to be some agreement about the status and the level of honesty of the information that is shared. If the mentor is from within the same organisation, it is particularly important that this subject be dealt with. For instance, if a learner reveals that he/she is seeking a new job without the knowledge of his/her line manager, do you, as mentor, owe it to the line manager to tell him/her? This needs to be carefully thought out. In general, the mentor should default to maintaining confidentiality in all circumstances where possible. But you do need an explicit agreement as to the boundaries.

What happens if a learner reveals information about a line manager who is sexually harassing a more junior female colleague? This is much more contentious, not only because it involves distress for somebody, but because it involves breaking the law as well. You need to have an agreement about what circumstances would cause you to break confidentiality.

Like all agreements, it should be a two-way process and should probably involve you guaranteeing confidentiality on things like commercially sensitive information.

Accessibility

We have already seen that learners value accessibility very highly, particularly for more dependent learners, who are likely to want, or even demand, more time than you have to give. It is worth discussing a reasonable and agreed allocation of time. This agreement may encompass not only how much time but when. It may also cover other aspects of communication. For instance, can learners call you at home on the telephone? Whatever the answer, both parties need to be clear and to agree what is reasonable.

Learning contract

Again, this may sound a little formal or legalistic and you may be more comfortable with the term 'agreement'. But like all relationships, the mentor–learner relationship is a two-way process. You are making an agreement and a commitment to give your time and expertise. What is the learner's part of the bargain? This may be more difficult to talk about, particularly in an informal or open-frame type of relationship. Nonetheless, you may reasonably expect learners, and it is a good discipline for them to learn, to make some commitments of their own.

If they are in a formal learning programme, this may involve delivering assignments or assessments, for instance, within certain agreed time scales. In other kinds of mentoring relationship it may just involve making a commitment to undertake certain activities in good faith.

141

Either way, there should be some objectives that surround the relationship, and both the mentor and the learner will need to be committed to deliver on these. This is better dealt with by an explicit agreement.

Boundaries

This is more of a 'catch all' phrase that covers a number of issues that are nonetheless important. It may cover the roles and mutual expectations of the relationship. It may cover the level of formality or professionalism expected by both parties. It may also deal with the boundary between friendship and work relationships.

All in all, the terms of reference, however formal or informal, give reasssurance to both mentors and learners that they understand what they can reasonably expect in terms of behaviour from each other. It should be established early on because it then provides a solid base from which to build the relationship into the next phase.

Setting objectives

It is important at the beginning of the relationship that the purpose is discussed and defined. For the learners, there are usually reasons why they need a mentor in the first place. These may be more or less specific, and may or may not be well articulated. One of the early conversations you should have is to explore what the learners' needs are and to try to develop a good understanding of them. These can then be treated as a set of standards, against which both the mentor and the learner can gauge their progress. In the first instance, though, they may be of quite a general nature and may involve statements like:

- Improving performance

- Developing a career

- Gaining support.

One of the jobs that the mentor can do is to help the learner to take these generalisations and turn them into specific objectives which are deliverable.

However, in almost any kind of mentoring relationship there will come a point where the learner decides upon or makes a commitment to some kind of plan or course of action. In these cases, setting objectives is a good discipline and is more likely to deliver a successful result.

Agenda

Having set out the basic or initial conditions under which a relationship will operate, you then need to think about what kinds of things are likely to come up for discussion. This is not setting an agenda in the formal sense, but just trying to mark out the basic areas of consideration for any mentor–learner relationship.

In the early part of the relationship the kinds of things that are most useful to discuss are:

- Breaking the ice

- Learning styles

- Terms of reference

- Setting objectives

- Mutual understanding of programme requirements

- Mutual understanding of roles

- Planning and action.

Phase II: Growth and performance
■ ■ ■

It is usually the case that if and when a relationship starts off correctly, it gathers its own momentum and carries on in quite a natural fashion. The suggested agenda we have set out for Phase I, if properly explored, would provide plenty to talk about for many months. There is no trigger or specific sign that marks a transition into this next phase. It is really a question of developing a fluency or fluidity in the way you go about things.

Once things start to move and to open out, it is rare that people need a formal or written agenda. The value of the agenda is as a checklist of possible topics to be considered, and as a lever to get things going. Once they are going, the substantive content of discussions arises quite naturally as a continuation of business as usual.

Phase II activity is marked by:

- Honest, trusting, sincere and open communication

- A focus on learning and growth

- Getting to grips with business issues

- Moving from plans to real outcomes.

But what do mentors do during this time? In fact, by this stage, the style and momentum usually carry both mentor and learner along quite naturally. The clues as to the individual tasks come from the four bases of the mentoring wheel. By way of summary, and collecting them together, here is a list of the kinds of task that a mentor will get involved in:

Mentoring tasks

- **Interpreter.** When necessary, the interpreter helps the learner to understand the nature and the workings of the organisation.

- **Advocate.** The advocate knows how to make things happen, get things done, and win understanding and support.

- **Maintaining a relationship.** Mentors establish and maintain a constructive and helpful relationship with the learner.

- **Process consultant.** A process consultant establishes a mutual understanding with the learner of how he/she will manage the learning process to achieve objectives, and how their relationship will support the learner.

- **Learning consultant.** He/she identifies and helps the learner to find and use learning opportunities.

(A comprehensive list of these tasks, together with indicators, can be found at the end of the book.)

The list can look quite daunting, but we have already mentioned that in fact, once the relationship starts to 'buzz', then each of these drops seamlessly into the agenda. However, there is a process to the conduct of the relationship. In its most general form, it takes the appearance of the model in Figure 10.

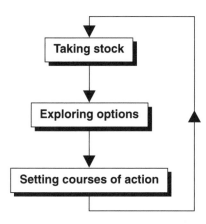

Fig 10 Model representing the conduct of a relationship

It is fairly easy to see that Figure 10 represents a typical management or problem-solving sequence. Therefore, it would be useful to examine here an approach to problem-solving in more detail. The reasons are twofold. First, it is a universally useful management process. Secondly, it is at the centre of a well-managed mentor–learner relationship.

Problem-solving

Much of the discussion between mentor and learner will involve an element of problem-solving. Problem-solving processes can be applied in a wide range of circumstances and situations. They may not necessarily be 'problems' in the normal sense of the word. The mentor–learner relationship will not necessarily be dominated by problems in the sense of things going wrong, but will involve substantially:

- 'How to'-type problems
- Dilemmas
- Puzzles
- Challenges
- Difficulties
- Blockages.

For all of these types of situation there needs to be a systematic approach. Therefore, it is useful for a mentor to have a proper range of problem-solving processes and skills.

A problem-solving model

In situations where there is an element of uncertainty – either about what has happened, or about how to go about something – then a systematic problem-solving approach is required in order to deliver a result.

We need a systematic approach to problem-solving because solving problems rarely happens in a single hit. Problem-solving is more than just waiting for the light to go on. It involves a systematic set of processes that need to be applied at various stages.

Problem solving is an ordered sequence of processes. Each stage is based on the asking of relevant questions and the collection and analysis of information. Merely learning or applying a set of mechanical rules will not solve difficult problems. They need to be used, but they do not replace other human skills and qualities, such as determination, creativity, intuition, and so on.

There are many problem-solving approaches available, but for convenience and coherence it is useful to use the basic set of processes that we set out for both counselling and coaching. These are:

- Define

- Describe

- Decide.

For a more generalised problem-solving approach, we can enhance it a little (see Figure 11).

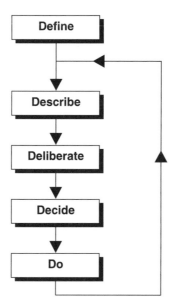

Fig 11   Model of a problem-solving approach

- **Define.** This involves a detailed statement and description of the problem.

- **Describe.** This involves identifying the major components of the problem and the relationships between them. It answers the question 'What is going on?' It is also the evaluation stage and involves the narrowing down or checking of hunches or hypotheses. It is a scientific process of testing and verification.

- **Deliberate.** This is the stage at which we build plans. It involves the generation and evaluation of options.

- **Decide.** Options are then selected.

- **Do.** The implementation phase.

There are convergent and divergent influences operating at different stages. This is useful to know because it changes our approach or thinking style. Let us look at an example.

147

HG has identified, through feedback, that his working relationships with subordinates are not very productive. This is a problem that he brings to a mentoring session to explore. Where do we start?

At the Define stage what we want to do is to get HG to state the problem as clearly as he is able (this may not be very clearly at all). Once he has been able to make a statement of the problem, he is then in a position to decide broadly what he wants to do about it. At this stage that doesn't mean that we have solved the problem, it just means that HG, for instance, will have decided that he wants an improvement in these relationships at work.

We then move on to the Describe phase. At this stage what we are doing is opening out and trying to make a map of the problem space. In the case of HG, we will be looking at what he does know about the situation. How does he go about dealing with subordinates? What does he think he does well? What doesn't he do so well? Are there certain situations or circumstances when things go wrong, or are more uncomfortable? Has he any ideas about what kinds of things he might be doing that other people see as a problem?

In this way we will be encouraging him to widen his perception of what is going on. We will also be getting him to try out certain kinds of explanation of the cause–effect processes involved. This stage is equivalent to trying to fit the pieces of the jig-saw together. We should not underestimate that this may be difficult for HG. There is a lot of personal sensitivity invested in these conversations. He may be more or less willing to examine his own behaviour through the eyes of others. Where things are very uncomfortable he may want to deny that there is any problem. In these circumstances, all we can do is give learners back the information that we have, check out interpretations, encourage them to check against reality, and possibly to challenge their interpretations.

Out of this exploration HG should develop, with our help, some ideas about what might be happening and why.

This then leads us naturally on to the next stage. What we do here is to check out our hunches and explanations against the real world. Moving through the Deliberate to the Decide stage may involve setting some objectives about trying new kinds of behaviour. Even before that, it might involve collecting some systematic information to support the explanations or hypotheses. One simple routine that is very under-used is that of going to ask people for some honest feedback.

What we are trying to do is to narrow down the field of explanations and then to test or verify them. A successful conclusion to this stage comes either when the explanation is complete and we understand what is happening, or when we have adjusted behaviour enough to have made progress.

In the final phase, we will be taking stock and deciding on future courses of action.

In the case of HG, it may be that it is only by the mentor challenging him and by him being brave enough to ask subordinates what they really feel, that he will come to an understanding that other people see his behaviour in a very different way from the way he does. One of the contributions that the mentor can make, as well as eliciting information and challenging the learner's perception, is in supporting the learner in devising and trying out new behaviours.

As we have said, not all mentoring situations will involve problems of this nature, but the processes of taking stock, setting courses of action, and checking the results is a universal approach that applies to nearly all of the activities that come under the mentoring umbrella.

Mentoring style

In this phase of the mentoring relationship, as the two partners grow together, so their individual styles and approaches will become apparent. As with any kind of relationship, the preferences and approaches of the individuals involved will determine the nature of the relationship. As mentors, we will all go about things in slightly different ways. Some mentors may be more 'up-front' or forceful. Others will be more relaxed and non-interventionist, and will be much more prepared just to sit and listen.

Some of the major factors that determine an individual's mentoring style are the following:

149

- Learning style
- Learner confidence
- Personality/personal style

These are not all separate and mutually exclusive factors. They do overlap, but nonetheless it is worth looking at each one in its own right.

Learning style

We have already looked in some detail at how learning style affects the approach of the individual when we covered the development base of the mentoring wheel. Equally, we looked at how the interplay of the learning styles of the mentor and learner affect the nature of the relationship. Making some judgements about an individual's approach is not just something to be done as a one-off at the first stage of the relationship. Because learning style can adjust as people widen their repertoire of behaviours, it should be re-visited and commented upon at regular intervals.

Learner confidence

We also mentioned the concept of learner confidence in looking at the development base of the mentoring wheel. Not unusually, learners will come into a relationship with a fairly low level of learner confidence. In unfamiliar circumstances they may well not take the lead in terms of setting their own objectives and taking responsibility for their own learning.

The key factor in mentoring style, as far as learner confidence is concerned, is the level of direction that the mentor provides. If the learners are naive learners and are at the low end of the confidence scale, they will be more dependent in their needs. They will see it as perfectly appropriate for a mentor to be quite directive. In fact, they may well almost demand it. Typical statements would be:

'When do you want me to do this by?'
'I am a bit disappointed – it's been too long since you got in touch.'

Notice that the responsibility here is being transferred from learner to mentor. This is typical for people with a low level of confidence. They will only gain confidence, bit by bit, as we feed them more and more responsibility. But initially, learners may need the mentor to take decisions for them.

At the other end of the scale, the highly confident learner will see it as inappropriate and unwelcome if the mentor is too directive. By definition, these people will be used to setting their own objectives and taking responsibility for themselves. They won't need the mentor to do it for them, so a much less directive style will be appropriate.

Personality/personal style

There is no evidence to suggest that any one style or type of personality makes a good mentor. In this sense, there is no 'identi-kit' picture of what a mentor should look like or how a mentor should behave. However, our investigation of the qualities of mentors does suggest that there are certain kinds of behaviour and approach that are better suited to the job. A key factor for the mentor is self-knowledge and self-awareness.

'I found it difficult to stop myself taking control and pushing others ...'

If we are aware of the way we go about things, then we are in a position to judge if it is appropriate and if it is working. We are also in a better position to make adjustments where necessary, because mentoring is also a learning experience for the mentor. Feedback, as much as communication, is a two-way process, and we must be constantly reading the situation and checking to make sure that what we are doing, and the way we are doing it, is okay.

Inasmuch as we know, there is a suggestion that good mentors will be more likely to be:

- Tender-minded rather than suspicious
- Experimental rather than apprehensive
- Self-sufficient rather than controlled
- Assertive rather than tense.

These should not be taken as selection (or de-selection) criteria, but rather as indicators of the preferences that learners have expressed, and therefore as characteristics to be emphasised where they are positive and limited where they are negative.

Phase III: Maturity

■ ■ ■

This stage of the process arrives when the relationship, and all of its attendant tasks and skills, becomes an unconscious competence. That is, it becomes automatic – we can do it perfectly well and we hardly have to think about it. In fact, for experienced managers and mentors, this might happen quite quickly.

Also, the nature of the mentoring relationship itself changes. It becomes very easy and comfortable. It often moves from the more professional or business-like relationship to a more friendly one.

151

It is always worth giving some thought to the ending or shifting of the relationship into another mode. If it is related to a particular programme, or to a particular set of circumstances, there will come a time when it will end in its current form. That ending needs to be dealt with thoughtfully. Relationships should not just cease. They should wind down in a planned way. In this way, the habit and reliance on that relationship can gradually be released over a period of time, rather than just stop.

■ Mentoring action point

As this chapter is a discussion of the key points involved in conducting a mentoring relationship, it gives a set of reference points to think about as you prepare to mentor. These are:

- Familiarise yourself with the mentoring tasks

- Familiarise yourself with the outline agenda for discussion

- Understand and be ready to use the problem-solving model

- Think about your natural mentoring style and whether it is appropriate.

'Mentors are also approachable on a wide range of issues, and they are comfortable to approach about personal as well as business issues.'

Chapter 9

■ ■ ■

The learners' experience

■ *Key learning points*

1 The experiences of learners can be explored through case studies.

2 The needs of learners need to be taken into consideration.

3 Learners need to be prepared for the mentoring experience.

4 Learners need to be able to cope with change and uncertainty.

So far, we have looked in some detail at mentoring from the point of view of the mentor, and to some extent from the point of view of the organisation. In order to round off our picture of mentoring, we should look at the concept through the eyes of the consumers of our mentoring – the learners. This should help us, as mentors, to understand what the issues and requirements are.

Most studies of mentoring report that learners gained a great deal from the experience.

But if we accept that such schemes do give a variety of benefits, we also need to know about the quality and the nature of the experience. We can start by listening to some individual stories.

■ CASE STUDY

BS – an operations manager

I have had two types of mentor – appointed mentors and champions. In both cases the relationship is the key element. Both must connect and empathise. They have to understand and behave as if it is a two-way process.

They must be open-minded and listen, but they must be willing to lead and direct as and when necessary. There must be respect and trust between the two partners. I have found also that no one mentor will necessarily provide the best or complete support for the individual. Mentors need to realise that interaction with peers and colleagues will also complement the mentoring.

When I mentor others I try to operate in a way in which I respond to positively myself. I would call this quiet persuasion. I am not sure that I provide the dynamic leadership that certain individuals require.

■ CASE STUDY

VP – a facilities manager

I would say that there is a difference between natural mentors and formal mentors. Natural mentors are more inclined to become a role model. They tend to offer support and advice without prompt as part of their normal behaviour. They tend to be highly regarded generally within the organisation/team or family. They are also approachable on a wide range of issues and they are comfortable to approach about personal as well as business issues.

Formal mentors, on the other hand, tend to operate in a structured approach, geared to achieving specific objectives. They are more focused and tend to be more limited to a range of advice – i.e. usually focused more on the task in hand.

In my experience, mentors need a high degree of perception to be able to understand individuals, as well as a supportive approach. They are sincere and confidential.

157

■ CASE STUDY

PK – a finance manager in the energy industry

I have had several mentors appointed for me and suffered frustrations such as insufficient time, unavailability and lack of interest in the subject matter. I don't think I have experienced 100 per cent satisfaction with any of them.

Mentors that I have sought out because I respect their opinions and values have proved of great benefit. One reason is because they are pleased with my seeking their opinion and help – it gives them a feeling of being valued.

There are people that have become my mentor/coach because they wanted to help me in my career. I have become very close personally to them, and we relate at all levels. I get very pleased when other people ask me to help them because that is a compliment. But I also find it difficult to stop myself taking control and pushing others.

■ CASE STUDY

KW – a manager in the construction industry

I remember a tutor at an FE college who guided me into teaching. They did it by example and by their strength of communication skills.

The team leader at my last job was also a mentor. I walked a line between someone with whom I would have a pint, and raised issues and sought advice from. Within the workplace a formal relationship resumed. It was never forced but always clearly understood.

In my present post, I look and learn and can, from a distance, gain insights from a new chief executive who displays many attributes that I admire. But there is no formal mentoring role.

I, myself, mentored a new teacher many moons ago. Years later we met – she's now a headmistress, and over a glass of wine she recounted the experience. She claims that the 'soft edge' philosophy/approach to the job that I provided gave her insights that she did not have as a very focused scientist. She claims to have learnt the social/human skills from that relationship.

■ CASE STUDY

BH – a manager in wine importing

I have had a number of experiences of mentoring. In my early career it was my manager who gave me advice, encouragement and permission to get on and do things.

In mid-career there was a director who was stimulating and encouraging. He was good at giving me the rope to try new things out. Later on I was mentored by the chairman. He brought real solid business experience and a kind of street wisdom. I also had a tutor for my DPhil who was very knowledgeable with a lot of know-how. He was a good motivator.

What learners want
■　■　■

The experiences recounted here are fairly typical of those people who have encountered mentoring in various forms over the years. It is also interesting to note that their experience encourages them to become mentors, and it also tells them how to mentor.

There are some points that come across quite strongly, and these are some of the most important. They are important because this is a bit of market research for mentors who want to know what learners want out of mentoring, and how they like mentors to go about it.

1 High level of interpersonal and communication skills

This is neither unusual nor unexpected. There is a clear need expressed here to form a close personal relationship, characterised by openness and trust and empathy. Terms such as 'approachable' and 'comfortable' also get some way towards this flavour that is so valued by learners.

Another element related to this is that the best mentors seem to be confident in talking about personal as well as work issues. This self-confidence enables them to move fluidly from one area of interest to another.

> *'Someone who I could "have a pint" with.'*
> *'I have become very close to them personally.'*

2 Need for respect and participation

There is frequent mention in personal accounts of mutual respect and the two-way aspect of mentoring relationships. The ability to listen seems to be very important in demonstrating this respect, but it also involves treating the other person as an equal, without reference to status.

> *'[Those] I have sought out because I respect their opinions and values have proved of great benefit.'*

3 Mentoring style

Good mentors seem to be able to put people at their ease. People describing good mentoring relationships report an uncanny mix between the comfortable and personal on the one hand and the professional and business on the other.

4 Role modelling

Time and again this aspect of mentoring gets mentioned. Learners choose mentors whom they respect, and whom they see as exemplars at what they do.

5 Availability

No surprises here. Learners always want time and they value mentors who can give it. An interesting thought, which is difficult to confirm, is that it always seems to be the best managers who are able to make time available.

6 Range of purposes

The sheer range of applications and contexts in which people have experienced mentoring or in which people are now trying mentoring is astonishing. They range from college applications to career functions and right the way through to general support.

7 The 'soft focus'

Quite often, either explicitly or, more usually, implicitly, it seems that learners are seeking more general or 'softer' skills, as well as the 'harder' skills or objectives. These include such things as changes in outlook, awareness, and so on. These kinds of objective are just as important, even if they are more difficult to pin down and to measure.

8 Value-added benefits

Quite often you hear of learners (and mentors too, for that matter) reporting benefits from the relationships that they had not anticipated. In one of our case studies, the quality of 'streetwise-ness' was mentioned as a case in point. In our case study on the National Mentoring Consortium, also mentioned above, 30 per cent of participants reported an improvement in their academic work – and this was not one of the explicit objectives of the pro-gramme.

It demonstrates that once people are in a positive or virtuous cir-cle of learning the benefits seem to ripple out like waves on water.

9 Motivation

Again, a fairly regular kind of report is that mentors are able to motivate and somehow 'gee up' the learners. Take the example in the case study below.

161

■ CASE STUDY

A day in the life of my mentor

(The Derby Mentor Project is a college-support project for Afro-Caribbean students.)

'Jill is my mentor. As I see it she is more than a positive role model. She is a veritable inspiration. She is black and a woman. Look beyond that and you find an intelligent, confident businesswoman.

I spent the whole day shadowing Jill and we went along to one of her meetings. We travelled to Loughborough to look at a potential site for a new development of the South Derbyshire Training and Enterprise Council. Jill is more than an educated black woman. She knows what she is talking about. She views everybody as her equal. This helped me to relax straight away. She is not too over confident, but confident enough to get the job done. Jill is a worthy opponent for anyone in her particular field, no matter which walk of life they come from. She is able to take the knocks as well as the praise, which in my opinion there is all too little of.

Jill has made me sit back, take a good look at myself and work harder towards my aspiration to become a writer. Like me, Jill is

▶

> *a single working mother, she has endless academic credits, and I am sure is held in high esteem by her colleagues. I am certain she will be of great help to me in my year with her as my mentor.*
>
> *In summary, all I can say about Jill and her achievements, is one word – GOSH!!!'*

Fears and uncertainties
■ ■ ■

We know a great deal in general about what learners say they want from mentoring relationships. The things on the wish-list are contained and wired into the mentoring wheel and into the list of skills, qualities and roles that go with it.

What those descriptions do not provide, though, is the list of things that are likely to make learners nervous or apprehensive. It is important for mentors to understand what the fears and anxieties of learners are, as they come into the relationship. Some of these reactions are natural and even functional, but they do need to be acknowledged and dealt with. In some cases, they can be anticipated and minimised, or even avoided. A planned and gentle induction, where confidence and trust develops, is likely to help people over any of these fears.

The kinds of anxiety that people have are listed below.

1 Fear of the unknown

The natural reaction for anyone who is faced with new situations or circumstances. Fear is too strong a word for most people (although not for some). It may be just nervousness or butterflies in the stomach. Slight discomfort will soon pass as learners are put at their ease, and they gain trust and knowledge of what is happening.

The sense of anticipation that we get is quite functional in that it is one of the things that enables us to raise our performance when faced with unusual circumstances. Mentors should see it as an opportunity to gain commitment and generate enthusiasm.

2 Fear of scrutiny

Learners may well come into a situation or relationship thinking that their deeper selves, their performance and their personality may be put under the microscope. The focus of discussions may well reach some fairly deep levels for learners quite quickly. They will be receiving feedback on their behaviour, how they are perceived by others, and their motives, values and capabilities may well be exposed.

In order to cope with this, they will need a high level of trust and reassurance that they will be treated respectfully and sensitively. It is often important for learners that they are not judged harshly – in fact a heavy judgemental approach is rarely helpful or appreciated.

3 Fear of failure

163

The context of many mentoring relationships involves an improvement in performance, knowledge and understanding, or changes of various sorts. People can easily get concerned about whether they will match up or cope. Some contexts, for instance, involve learners writing reports, assignments or projects. Many fear that their ability in this area is poor, and so they feel very vulnerable.

Equally, where applications involve developing skills, it is natural to worry that we may not perform as well as we would like. In short, it is possible that people will be faced with the limitations of their own capability. This needs to be confronted with a great deal of sensitivity. For a mentor, the first thing is to anticipate. Then we should be checking for people's reactions. Remember that much of the information people give about their mood or inner state is non-verbal, so mentors need to be good at interpreting this.

4 Fear of the relationship

In the first instance, a learner (and a mentor) will wonder how the relationship will work out. This is perfectly natural. It happens to us all in novel circumstances. Think about the last time you started a new job, and the thoughts you had just before you met your new boss, or colleagues or team.

Such fears, for most people, are not likely to be disabling – particularly if mentor and learner are already acquainted. However, the sooner the ice is broken the sooner such apprehensions recede.

As with all of these fears, a mentor should follow the stages:

- Anticipate

- Check

- Acknowledge

- Adjust

- Reassure.

Preparing learners for mentoring

■ ■ ■

How can we prepare learners for mentoring? We would like them to come having prepared some ideas that they want to discuss. However, this may not always be the case.

It also begs the question of whether learners should receive some form of induction. On a planned or structured scheme, learners are quite likely to receive some form of briefing or induction. Where the driving force for the relationship rests with the individuals, this is less likely to be the case. If there has been no induction to the programme, then the learner and mentor together should incorporate this into their own work together.

The induction into the relationship should be considered separately. One key variable here is how well, if at all, the mentor and learner know each other at the outset. If they know each other very little, then this is the obvious starting place.

The induction itself may not happen before the relationship begins, so it may need to be incorporated into Phase I of the life cycle (see Chapter 8). Some of the items that learners might think of before the first meeting, or early on, are:

- SWOT analysis of professional, technical and personal skills

- Briefing/information on the context or application

- Some initial thoughts on the roles and expectations of themselves and those they have of the mentor

- Who else they might want or need to talk to or inform

- Some ideas on terms of reference

- Note down some basic biographical information about themselves to share with the mentor

- Hopes, fears, aspirations, questions.

It may be that this is too formidable a list to give a learner as preparation for a first meeting – it needs to be a slow, comfortable start in the first instance. If we want to give them something to think about that is a mind-size chunk, and that won't frighten them off, then the following is about right:

- What would they like to get from the relationship?

- Biographical information to share.

Change
■ ■ ■

One of the reccurent themes in our exploration of the world as seen through the eyes of a learner is dealing with the notion of change. It is important to give some thought about what makes it difficult, and about how to deal with it.

We know that people can change more readily from a base of security. As people feel more secure, they are more confident in being able to try things out without feeling threatened.

However, people have a great deal invested in their current approaches and ways of dealing with the world and behaviour. It has usually served them very well over a long period of time. Even when it seems less than useful, it has some sense and use for them. If we then start to knock down the fabric of people's lives by taking some bricks out of the wall, it can be very threatening.

So how should mentors approach the notion of change for learners? What kinds of strategy should be employed? The following considerations should prove useful.

1 Do they want to change?

The motivation and the need for change must come from the individual concerned. This arises not when we tell them, but when they become aware that current habits or approaches are limiting, or that there are opportunities to do things differently or better. Our role as a mentor is as a guide through that awareness-raising process.

2 Do they know what they want?

People are often not ready for change until they have a clear picture or vision of what the alternative is. We can assist by helping them to explore possibilities and opportunities in a protected environment. We can challenge the suitability, feasibility and acceptability of proposed changes.

3 Are they ready for change?

Is the motivation strong enough? Have they thought it through? Sometimes, people can get to the point of knowing that they need to change and even defining what that change might be. These are rational processes. Then the less rational, more human fears and blocks appear. This is a natural stage, but is only a stage.

Have you ever had the experience of making a major personal purchase, like a car or a home? You go through all of the sensible steps, including gathering information, making choices and so on. Then, when the day comes to sign the contract, you get a sudden panic. What happens if it all goes wrong?

We often need to retrace some of our steps until we have the confidence and reassurance to make the final leap. A process of rehearsal, scrutiny and anticipation by thought experiments is often needed. Mentors need to be aware that for some people it can take a lot of time and reflection before a learner is really ready for the next step.

There are also some individuals whose personal style is to 'jump' before they are ready. This is related to the learning styles (see Chapter 6). In these cases, a mentor can help by checking that the learners have gone through the appropriate planning and preparing stages. The learning cycle can be a good model to use as a basis for such preparation.

4 Is the first step modest enough and actionable?

Where people are tackling change – particularly major change – they may well need it to be broken down into mind-sized chunks. Every journey starts with the first step, and planning on the basis of a series of small but actionable steps is a good way to approach change.

167

By using these steps we can make change less frightening and formidable and easier to tackle than would otherwise be the case.

What happens if things go wrong?
■ ■ ■

Whatever plans we make and however seriously we approach the job of mentoring, there is always the possibility that things will not work out. For individuals this can be distressing, particularly as it may not be anyone's fault. In a corporate scheme, the programme manager will need some methods, both for monitoring what goes on and for dealing with problems, if and when they occur.

It is worth saying that it is rare for things to go wrong, as such, although it is less rare for things not to work as well as they might. This latter case is more likely to happen in schemes where mentors are appointed for learners, rather than self-selected.

However, we need to be realistic and aware that things can go wrong for a number of reasons. Here are some of the most usual.

- **Chemistry.** There can be a clash of personalities or styles, or for some other reason it just doesn't work between two people. For such cases, there should be a 'no fault–no blame' exit arrangement.

- **Conflict of roles.** The most common cause of conflict is where line managers are appointed as mentors, but it can also happen that the standing or line responsibilities can cause a conflict of interest for the mentor.

- **Mentor too forceful or directive.** The style of the mentor may just not be 'soft' enough for the learner.

- **Mentor won't listen.** In some rare cases the mentor is unable to adjust to the new role, and doesn't check whether his/her approach is acceptable.

- **Lack of skills.** Sometimes a mentor just does not have the appropriate skills for the job. In rare cases, this may relate to the skills sets in the interpersonal or development bases of the mentoring wheel. More often, it is because the requirements of the context or application are too detailed, specialised or demanding.

- **Learner contribution.** Sometimes it can be the case that the learners fail to deliver on their part of the bargain. This can happen with naive learners who approach the relationship with a very dependent mind-set. If they expect a lot from the mentor but don't contribute themselves, a mentor can legitimately lose patience.

If the mentor does not know the learner before the mentoring begins, then listening, exploring and checking are the order of the day. If things are not going as well as they might, then some diagnostic skills are required. Both mentor and learner should be mature and self-aware enough to be able to discuss problems and be willing to tackle them. Usually, only minor adjustments are needed to put a relationship back on track.

There must be space and legitimate opportunity for learners to express themselves. Mentors should not be put off if comments do seem negative. Remember, the mentors should also be able to see themselves through the eyes of the learners, and may receive feedback on their own approach and style. They have to be 'big' enough to take that. Hopefully, the correct spirit of positive and helpful feedback will have been created and both can accept this philosophically.

In summary then, there are some clear points that come out of any examination of the experiences of learners – both positive and negative. The greatest sensitivities seem to be related to the ways that mentors conduct themselves. The qualities which have been stressed throughout this book are:

- Sensitivity

- Empathy

- Perception.

The softer or more human qualities seem to be valued above the more professional or work-based skills. Or, to put it another way, without these qualities, the mentoring experience does not seem to be as rich or rewarding for the learners.

169

The potential sensitivity or vulnerability of learners in some mentoring contexts cannot be over-emphasised, and mentors should be prepared to deal with these.

■ *Mentoring action point*

- Think about the world through the eyes of the learners. What do you think they want out of the relationship? Now check!

- Make a list of the five or six key points from this chapter that you should bear in mind as a mentor.

- Use the ideas here to induct your learner slowly into the relationship and prepare for it.

'... the visible commitment of the top management means a great deal to the organisation as a whole, and to the participants in particular.'

Chapter 10

■ ■ ■

Mentoring programmes

■ *Key learning points*

1 There are key features which should be included in setting up an in-company or sponsored scheme.

2 We examine the key ideas behind the selection and training of mentors.

3 Mentoring programmes must be properly implemented and evaluated.

In this chapter we will look at the ideas involved in managing programmes in organisations. In the organisation base of the mentoring wheel we looked at the influence of the organisation on individual mentoring relationships. Here, we move the focus from the individual relationship to the organisation itself. The key questions that we will be looking at include:

- How to plan and set up an in-company or sponsored programme?

- What are the key factors in running and managing such a programme?

- What are the potential pitfalls?

- How do we evaluate in-company programmes?

174

In many ways, a mentoring programme is no different from any other initiative or project within an organisation. There are some differences because of the particular nature and scope of such a project, but it should still be tackled like any other management task.

There can be a temptation to assume that because mentoring is a personal issue between the two participants, then the organisation should take a 'hands-off' approach. This is only true to a certain extent. It is true that the exchange between the individuals involved should be a free one, with little or no external interference. However, the organisation should be involved in a positive and practical way in a number of dimensions. Of these, there are three that stand out:

- **Resourcing.** The organisation can support a programme by committing resources to it. Chief among these will be staff time, effort and contribution.

- **Management infrastructure.** Another way that a programme can be supported is by the application of management processes to set it up, maintain it and keep it running successfully.

- **Endorsement.** This one may be less obvious, but in fact it can be the most important. Commitment can be an essential symbol and there are many practical and simple ways that it can be demonstrated.

■ CASE STUDY

A management development programme in the construction industry

A major supplier to the construction industry decided upon an in-company programme to develop its first-line and middle managers. As so often, many of them had achieved promotion through technical or functional skills, and had learnt the business of management by picking it up along the way rather than in any systematic structure.

Pressures from the external market place, together with internal pressures to devolve responsibility and decision-making and develop a more responsive and entrepreneurial approach, had created a need to support the development of managers in a structured programme. It was decided that the individual managers would be supported by mentors to help them through the programme and to maximise the benefits of the programme.

Great importance was placed on the programme, and selection for the programme was quite competitive. To reinforce this importance, it was decided that the directors themselves would be the mentors. However, directors were not to mentor those in their direct line of responsibility. Rather, they were to mentor cross-functionally, so widening the perspective of the learners and facilitating cross-functional understanding and communication. It worked as shown in Figure 12.

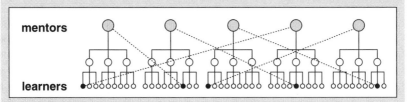

mentors

learners

Fig 12   Cross-function mentoring relationships

Another interesting feature was that the learners and the mentors received some third-party support. Because of the technical and demanding nature of the particular programme, the external provider supplemented the internal mentoring with external mentoring support for those detailed aspects of the programme that the mentors would find it most difficult to get to grips with. Thus there was a division of labour between the internal and external mentors.

The internal mentors would be facilitators, who would support the learners, help them to monitor progress and set goals. They would contribute their knowledge of the organisation and of the business environment, and act as coaches where necessary or appropriate.

The external mentors would deal with the particular requirements of the programme, in terms of the content and the outputs.

176

Three things can be learned from this particular experience. First, the visible commitment of the top management means a great deal to the organisation as a whole, and to the participants in particular. Secondly, there is a great deal to be gained from mentoring cross-functionally. Not only does it add value for the individual learners, but it takes out of the relationship any potential role conflict because it is not in the line. Thirdly, we see a movement here from the notion of an individual mentor to the wider notion of mentorship. In sophisticated environments, individuals can, where they are encouraged, define their own mentoring needs and seek out those individuals who can satisfy those needs. And, of course, that need not be a single individual.

Another feature of the case study programme that is worth remarking upon is the intervention of an outside agency. In this case, it came about because the development itself was provided by the supplier as well as a component of the mentoring. The more usual case is for the totality of a programme to be driven and run internally. As this is the most usual model, we should look at some of the key features of such programmes.

Setting up a mentoring programme
■ ■ ■

Although the delivery of an internal mentoring programme is quite different from many other projects and initiatives at work, the setting up and the other management aspects are very similar. The key aspects to be considered are:

- Defining the aims or purposes
- Planning and resourcing
- Selecting and training mentors
- Monitoring and evaluating

Defining the aims or purposes

There is an important balancing act to be achieved here. On the one hand, there will be an organisational context and a set of organisational purposes that surround the mentoring programme. These will clearly influence, if not define, the purposes of the programme. There will also be a set of purposes which will be entirely internal to the mentoring programme. In other words, the mentoring will serve some greater purpose for the organisation concerned. There need not be any conflict in these sets of purposes. There are huge areas in a healthy organisation where the interests of the individuals and the interests of the organisation coincide.

177

However, what may be more difficult is to prescribe exactly what the outcomes will be for any individual relationship. We will deal with this also when we come to evaluating mentoring activity (see page 182).

What is necessary at this stage is to define the broad thrust of the programme so that it can be communicated to, and shared by, the participants. These broad purposes usually involve development, learning, skills, competence, understanding or attitude.

It is possible, depending on the context, for the purposes to be much more specific. Supporting people on internal or external development programmes would provide very clear and specific purposes. Positive action programmes to increase the participation of women or people from ethnic minorities in management would also fall into this category, and would thus also require very specific and quantified ways of measuring the success of the mentoring intervention.

If the purposes are highly specific, and are to be met in a structured programme, this will form the context base of the mentoring wheel. A method for providing a description of a mentoring context or application was provided in Chapter 5 on the uses of mentoring.

Planning and resourcing

Planning involves defining the major dimensions of the programme itself. The first requirement is to think about who will be involved. From what area or level in the company will the participants come? There are also some options about who is involved. Will they be volunteers? Will they be invited? Will they be selected?

If participants are to be selected, there need to be some criteria for selection, not just for the purposes of sensible logistical management of the programme, but also to act as a reference point for the broad purposes specified at the last stage. Therefore, a process by which candidates are brought into the programme may need to be introduced.

As always, anticipation and planning are key. If selection is open, what happens if 200 volunteers turn up rather than the 20 expected? If participants are to be selected, what happens to those who are not selected? This sort of communication is meaningful in a political environment, which all organisations are, and mismanagement of it can cancel out any accrued benefit from the programme itself. In short, a planning process needs to take place and there need to be staff to oversee it. In our experience, the role of a champion or project manager is a key feature of successful programmes. There are two kinds of champion for an in-company or sponsored programme.

The first is the role-model champion. Role-model champions tend to be involved by doing it visibly, and so lead and set an example

178

for others. They tend to be involved in the design and development of the programme, and often have a significant personal investment in the success of the programme.

The other is the project-manager champion. A project-manager champion's contribution tends to come by being at the centre of the mentoring wheel. He/She is often a programme coordinator, who knows everyone and whom everyone knows. He/She is likely to be the central source of information and advice.

Also at this stage, the timetable needs to be planned. The key features that need to be planned are:

- Selection and induction of participants/learners

- Selection training/induction of mentors

- A programme timetable if the mentoring is not open-framed

- Support for mentors

- Definition of monitoring processes

- Proper exit processes.

179

A number of these features need some explanation. We will cover the training and induction of mentors below, but mentors may also need some ongoing information and support. There need to be systems and processes in place to keep the whole thing turning over. There should be some form of feedback loop from the mentoring experience back to the mentors.

We know that mentors are there to support the learners, but it is often forgotten that mentors themselves need support. Sometimes this is just information about what is happening, but it can be more than this. If the individuals and the organisation are to learn from the mentoring experience, there needs to be some mechanism to share good experience and practice. Similarly, mentors need somewhere to turn when they themselves need advice or support. Accumulated experience shows quite strongly that mentors value the opportunity to network and to share experiences.

> **■ CASE STUDY**
>
> ## A local government manager
>
> *'I felt at first that I was thrown in at the deep end. It was more or less a case of – here's your protégé, now get on with it. It wasn't that I didn't think that I had the skills, or anything like that, it was more that I wasn't really sure what we were both supposed to be doing.*
>
> *If I'm honest, I was also worried that I would make a hash of it. It can be quite daunting not knowing what is expected of you. What made it a little easier was that the protégé was more nervous than me at the first meeting.*
>
> *Once we got going it was okay, but there were times when I could have done with some advice myself on a few matters. There was no real agreement on things like how much time we should spend, and so on. In the end, we worked it all out as we went along, and it has not put me off at all.*
>
> *But I would recommend strongly that mentors are given some kind of introduction and some sort of ground rules to operate with – even if it is just to get you off on the right foot.'*

Another important planning and resourcing feature is the need to provide back-up or solutions when partnerships don't work out. We have already stressed the need for some kind of 'opt-out' clause for both mentors and learners. The organisation, through its project management, needs to provide and enable solutions to such problems.

Selecting and training mentors

Once the purposes have been defined and the context described, it should be possible, using the tools provided in this book, to describe the key roles, skills and attributes that the mentors will need. The selection processes should be designed by the organisation to best suit the needs identified. In our experience, volunteers always make the best mentors. It is only in this way that the correct orientation and commitment can be expected. Similarly, we have discussed in some detail the relative merits of line managers being mentors.

This leads on, then, to the issue of induction, briefing or training. The training of mentors usually involves two components. The first one is in relation to the context itself. It is important that prospective mentors have the basic information, but also that they understand the context, and are in tune with it.

The second component involves the skill sets of the other bases of the mentoring wheel. The skills that are associated with the interpersonal and the development bases are critical. Mentors should be selected either because they already possess these skills, or they must be trained to develop these skills. Careful selection can minimise the need for training input. Another alternative is to see this as an opportunity to provide a development experience for the mentors themselves.

Another component that should be considered at this stage is that of terms of reference and modes of operation. Prospective mentors will be keen to know, and should receive answers on, some basic questions at this stage.

■ How often should we meet?

■ How much time should be given?

■ What are the criteria?

Failure to answer these questions will result in a loss of confidence and credibility in the programme from the outset. The answers to such questions may not be definitive, of course, and for good reasons. This ambiguity can be dealt with in two ways. It can be dealt with in a set of guidelines that are given at an early stage (induction or training), when mentors can question them. Alternatively, they can be arrived at formatively by discussion, negotiation and experience. Many successful programmes set out with very little by way of prescription, and run on the good will and good faith of the participants and their learned experience. However, the more that can be set out in the beginning, the better. The issues certainly need an opportunity to be discussed.

In summary, then, good training programmes will usually cover:

- The objectives and processes of the context or application

- The roles and skills of mentoring, as appropriate to the context

- The guidelines, or terms of reference.

Once mentors are selected and trained, the next stage is to match the mentors to the learners. This is not always as easy as it might seem. It is possible to set up criteria. These might include:

- Location

- Function or technical specialism

- Gender

- Business unit.

182

Such a logical matching process incorporates the assumption that the organisation will make the choice. In many circumstances, particularly where the mentors and learners don't know each other, this may be a sensible approach. Where mentors and learners are likely to know each other, the best approach is to operate an open choice. However, this can result in logistical or political problems. In such cases, there should at least be the offer of a veto.

Monitoring and evaluating

The organisation needs to set up a system of monitoring the mentoring activity. There are a number of basic reasons for this. The first is to ensure that all is well. This involves checking that participants are developing appropriate and productive relationships, and that things are happening as they are supposed to. The second reason is to ensure that the proposed benefits are being delivered for all concerned. A further reason is to capitalise on and learn from the shared experience.

There are a number of issues, however, that make evaluating a mentoring programme difficult in some ways. A key question is whether you evaluate a programme or scheme from the perspective of the individuals involved or of the organisation and its goals and objectives. The answer, of course, is both – where possible or appropriate.

Evaluation at the organisational level can only be done if the objectives or goals were specific and measurable in the first place. In the case of the positive action programmes for women managers, there is a clear means of measuring success. However, on a second look, it may not be so clear or as simple as it seems. The easy solution would seem to be to count the number of women managers before and after. However, this may involve a number of difficulties. On the one hand, you cannot control the other variables – to be sure that all the women promoted were as a direct result of the programme. Although, if, at some time in the future, there are significantly more women managers, then the programme would probably be deemed to be a success, quite reasonably. On the other hand, how long would you have to wait to do such a measurement? It could take a considerable time before such a measurement would make sense.

183

In such cases, the expected and desired outcome would be enough in itself, even if it were not possible to quantify that success. It should also be remembered that mentoring is an additive model, so that any success can be considered a bonus, as to do it does not necessarily compete with other priorities.

Another potential problem with evaluating mentoring schemes against organisational criteria is the ownership of the information. What information can the organisation reasonably expect or require from the participants? In some cases, the organisation may have to compromise on the information it receives in order to maintain the integrity of the confidentiality between mentors and learners.

The most usual way to evaluate outcomes from mentor–learner relationships is to look internally at the relationships themselves. There are a number of methods that can be used here:

- **Questionnaires.** These can be used by both mentors and learners to evaluate the benefits of the experience. If anonymity is guaranteed, then some quite rich information can be captured about the quality and the benefits of the relationships. Judgements can also be made about the strength of the mentoring infrastructure. Quite often, the evaluation of the relationships themselves is only one component of the evaluation of the programme, particularly if the mentoring is only one component of the programme as a whole.

- **Interviews.** These can provide rich and in-depth qualitative information about all aspects of the mentoring relationships, and the programme as a whole.

- **Group discussion.** This is a very good way of sharing ideas. It can also be interactive and developmental, so that ideas that emerge can be enhanced, explored in depth and new ideas can be developed.

We can make a useful distinction here between two different kinds of programme.

The Hi-key programme

This is where the organisation takes a very visible lead in the programme. The objectives tend to be very specific and tend to be external to the individual relationship, reflecting the needs of the organisation to a high degree. A good example would be a fast-track graduate management development programme. The outcomes here, although clear for the individuals involved, would also be measurable for the organisation – in this case, graduates at particular stages of their development. A slightly different example would be a programme to support project managers. The successful delivery of the projects themselves would be the yardstick.

The Lo-key programme

This is where the organisation takes on a much less visible and more hands-off role. It may draw up some broad parameters, but its role is basically facilitative and supportive. The objectives are set mainly with reference internally to the relationship and mainly in terms of benefit to the individual learner. Organisations that are seeking broader, more diffuse aims, such as cultural change or developing learning within the organisation, are more likely to favour the lo-key approach.

What is interesting is that in a huge range of programmes, across different sectors of industry and across the range of possible uses and applications, mentoring relationships have received strong endorsement from learners. It is the exception where this has not been the case, and this has usually occurred when something has gone wrong.

When programmes have been evaluated, the benefits to learners would be predicted and expected. What is less often expected are the benefits for the mentors themselves, which are also typically reported. These can be considered as a bonus.

What can go wrong?

▪ ▪ ▪

With the best will in the world, sometimes things do go wrong. In the last chapter we have looked at the kinds of things that can go wrong from the perspective of the learner, and from the internal perspective of the relationship. It is worth considering what sorts of things might go wrong from the perspective of the organisation, or from the external perspective of the programme as a whole. The major pitfalls relate to many of the points made above and include:

- **Lack of planning or management.** Where assumptions are made that goodwill will triumph over all contingencies, there may well be problems. Lack of training and lack of ongoing support for mentors are key reasons.

- **Selection.** This happens where somehow the 'wrong' mentors have been chosen for the programme. It is not necessarily the same as poor matching of mentors to learners since this is a problem that can usually be overcome.

- **Lack of support within the organisation.** In practice, this usually means a lack of support from the top management within the organisation. Where this is missing, there is often a lack of leverage, a lack of credibility or a perceived lack of value.

- **Politics.** This is quite a difficult one to pin down, but mentoring relationships operate outside the normal line man-

185

agement and control systems of an organisation. As such, they by-pass much of the normal political control and the power structure. This can cause resentments and blocking activities from vested interests.

- **Culture.** There are organisations and cultures where mentoring-type relationships just go against the grain of accepted practice. As such, these newer types of relationship can be obstructed and marginalised.

This leads us on quite naturally to state some of the key elements to running a successful programme. Apart from the components of good practice set out above, the following seem to be consistently associated with successful programmes:

- Visible top management support
- Careful selection of mentors

- Training and induction of mentors
- A champion or project manager
- Sharing of, and learning from, experience.

By way of summary, we set out below a programme or checklist for the implementation of a programme or scheme within an organisation.

■ Implementation checklist

1	Is the organisation ready and capable?
2	Have aims and goals been defined?
3	Is there commitment from the top and is this visible?
4	Has a champion or project manager been appointed?
5	Are there criteria for selecting mentors?
6	Are there criteria for selecting learners?
7	Are the mentors to be trained?
8	Is there a system for matching mentors and learners?
9	Have terms of reference been set and guidelines given?
10	Are there systems for monitoring and evaluating in place?
11	Are there contingency plans to deal with problems?

■ *Mentoring action point*

- Familiarise yourself with the five keys to a successful programme

- Ensure that you are clear about your own role in any programme you become involved in

- Use the processes defined here to check that your programme has covered all of the bases

- Use the 'One Stop Mentor' section on page 203 to reflect on and develop your own role and your own programme

- You should try to capture some of the key personal learning points for yourself from the whole book. A mind map may be useful here, or you may find the 'One Stop Mentor' section on page 203 can help.

187

'Just do it!'

Chapter 11

■ ■ ■

Getting started

■ *Key learning points*

1   We set out the main practical considerations for new mentors.

2   The 10 keys to successful mentoring are a useful reference.

3   How to go about some important mentoring issues.

In this final chapter we will look at the key questions that new mentors have on becoming mentors for the first time. Although people may have been involved in coaching, counselling and supporting staff and colleagues for many years as part of the natural flow of work, they may still be nervous when they are asked to mentor someone for the first time.

This might be because the term mentoring suggests something entirely different from those things that they are used to doing. It might be because people interpret mentoring as a role that they should fulfil rather than as a familiar set of processes. In other words, there can be a mystique about the term which leads people to think it is very different to what it actually is. Along with this, many people will have the pessimistic notion that everybody else knows what it is but they don't. Of course, this is rarely the case.

Another potential problem is that mentoring usually happens in a context. There is a set of purposes, and again, the mentor in the first instance may not know exactly what these are. All of these things can add up to some confusion, and they can induce some anxiety in the potential mentor.

What we shall do in this chapter is to take the ten areas that potential or new mentors focus on when asking questions about mentoring. These areas or sets of questions are not usually about the theoretical or philosophical aspects of the concept. New mentors are much more likely to wonder about what to do tomorrow morning, the first time they see their learner, than they are to worry about the finer aspects of the definition of the term.

Sometimes it is these smaller, practical details that worry people most and prevent them from feeling positive and comfortable about the role. The chapter is organised into the ten areas that seem to be of most concern, so that it can be used as a reference section, to dip into as and when necessary.

We finish off with the 'How do I ...' section, that gives a checklist for each of the most asked-about methods or processes in mentoring.

Me

■ ■ ■

Perhaps the most important thing is to prepare yourself so that you feel comfortable in the role. If you aren't comfortable then the relationship may not develop as easily or productively as it should, and your learner may pick up on your apprehension. Remember, the learner too may be apprehensive, and it is part of your role to support and reassure them.

The keys to preparing yourself are:

- **Find out as much as you can about the context.** Is it driven by the organisation? If it is, there will be some information – either written or as a briefing/induction. If the individual has approached you directly, ask what they are intending to do and to achieve, and what information they can give you.

- **Find out about the aims/purposes.** They may be a 'given'. That is, there is some statement of pre-defined purposes. If not, don't worry, it just becomes part of the conversation the first time you meet.

- **Other mentors.** Have other people done this before, or are there others doing it now, also for the first time? Either way, find out who they are and talk to them. This will provide useful information, but also a means of support for you.

- **Self management.** Do you have time to do this? How much time do you have, or are you willing to give? Is that time during work, or after work? Does the time come in one hour slots, or half day slots? What about time on the phone?

191

Them

■ ■ ■

The key questions here are what do you know about them, and what do you need to know about them? This is relevant whether you already know them or if you don't. If you don't know them, getting some information to begin to build a picture is a help in preparing yourself. If you do know them already, you need to be aware that there is a good deal that you don't know about them.

This will be a new kind of relationship, and you will share different kinds of knowledge of each other.

- If you don't know them, try to find out the bare minimum biographical information: which organisation; which business unit; job role; gender; age and so on. A CV would be useful.

- If you do know them, adjust your perception of them by finding out at least one thing that you didn't already know about them. A CV would be useful.

- Did they choose to come on the programme? Did they choose you as mentor? If they didn't, and they know you – are they happy with the assignment?

- Why are they undertaking this programme or seeking mentoring support?

The Organisation

The nature of the organisation always affects a mentoring relationship, whether it is in an active or a more passive way. What role it will play, and how supportive it will be are important considerations.

- Is this part of an organisation driven programme? If it is – what is the scope and what are the aims and objectives? What is the involvement of the organisation, and do they place any requirements or boundaries on the relationship? Do they respect your contribution and will they support this in terms of time and other resources?

- If this is an organised programme, try to find out the scope and nature of the programme. Are there any guidelines for mentors?

Line manager

It is always better if the line manager is informed and supportive of the relationship. You should check what they know, and what they need to know, and anticipate if there are likely to be any problems.

- Who is the line manager of your learner? Have they been consulted? Do they approve?

- What do they know about the purposes of the mentoring relationship?

- Can you arrange a tri-partite meeting to discuss the issues?

- Will they be inclined to give the learner scope for development activities at work?

- What, if anything, do they want to know – at the outset, or during the course of the relationship?

First session

■ ■ ■

The first time you meet can be a time of nervousness or apprehension on both parts. This can be dealt with by good preparation. Remember, the first time you meet may set the mood and the ethos for the future of the relationship.

- Who takes the initiative – you or them?

- Where do you meet – in work or out of work? Do you go to them or do they come to you?

- Agree how long the first meeting will be in advance. It is a good discipline to show that you are going to time manage the meetings productively from the start.

- Prepare a list of three or four things to talk about to get the conversation going. Make these fairly neutral in the first instance so that you can break the ice, and make the learner comfortable.

- Prepare a short introduction to yourself – tell them a few things about you as well. Try to anticipate what they might want to know.

- Remember 66:33. Be prepared to listen more than you talk.

- Remember that they may be more nervous than you.

The agenda

It is good practice to discuss and get some broad agreement early on about the basic dimensions of the sessions – what you are going to talk about, what you are going to tackle, and so on.

- Look at the outline agenda in Chapter 8. It should give you some ideas on the broad areas for discussion.

- Are your sessions going to be general, free-flowing discussions, or are they going to be more structured? Are they going to be active sessions, involving coaching or specific content?

- Seek agreement on what each session is going to be about at the outset.

- Who takes charge, or takes the lead in setting the agenda? You may need to make some judgements about the confidence of the learner to do this.

- Should I keep records?

- Will I have to make assessments or decisions about the performance of the learner in any way?

Style

What the sessions will be like is an important consideration for both parties. To some extent the style will emerge and develop over a period of time. However, you will both have ideas and interests in the style in which the relationship will be conducted. It is a defining component of the relationship and it should develop to suit both of you.

- Will the sessions be formal or informal?

- Will they be structured or not?

- Does the learner need a directive or a low key style?

- How much responsibility or initiative will the learner take, and how much will they want or need me to take?

- How much do you know about your own style or approach?

Do you 'tell' or interpret strongly, or are you naturally non-interventionist?

Learning

Since learning and development are a major focus of any mentoring relationship, you need to feel confident about your role and responsibilities as a developer of people.

- Think about your own development by focusing on how you have learnt and developed over the years. Has this been through courses, books or work experiences and activities?

- Familiarise yourself with the learning cycle.

- What does your learner know about his/her own learning needs?

- How long is it since he/she has done any systematic learning?

- Talk to them explicitly about their own learning experiences, preferences and style.

195

Coaching vs counselling vs mentoring
■ ■ ■

People can get confused about some of the fine differences and distinctions between these. Sometimes people have experience of one or another of these, and want to know – how is mentoring different?

- Think about your own coaching and/or counselling experience. List and describe the skills that you have, and think about these as strengths.

- Where you think you need to know more, search out books, information or courses to help you.

- Don't be afraid to talk to other people who have the relevant skills or experiences, and to pick their brains.

- Use the chapters of this book to help you with the distinctions between these disciplines.

- Most of all – don't worry! Most of what you will need will come naturally, with practice. Don't try to convince yourself or your learner that you are perfect. Discuss your own strengths and development needs.

Support
■ ■ ■

Mentors don't enter into relationships perfectly equipped and perfectly formed. They have their own development needs, and they should expect to learn themselves from the experience. As with anybody else, they may need help, advice and support in doing this.

- Who mentors you? Identify at least one other person to whom you can turn for advice.

- Network. Get to know other mentors and talk to them – either about past experience, or to share ideas about the current situation.

- Find out if there are set procedures or arrangements for various contingencies. If there are problems, or if you reach a point where your learner needs a kind of help or resource that you do not have access to, identify where you might find this.

- If you are working within a set programme, why not talk to someone who has been mentored on the programme. What was their experience, and what did they need?

- Keep a note of problems, queries or questions that you need to deal with. In this way you are more likely to remember them and deal with them.

How do I ...?
■ ■ ■

A great deal of the questions that prospective or new mentors have take the form of 'What happens if ...?', or 'How do I ...?'. This final section seeks to give some advice on the common questions of that type.

How do I show I am interested

Showing interest is a key set of skills which provide a platform for developing a productive relationship.

- Remember 66:33. Listen more than you talk.

- Ask open questions.

- Watch for body language clues, acknowledge and respond.

- Talk about them – their interests and problems.

- Show sensitivity.

- Don't rush – be prepared to slow down.

- Be flexible – don't just stick to business issues.

How do I check that I am doing all right?

197

You will want to know that what you do is benefiting the learner and making a difference. How can you ensure things are going well?

- Ask them!

- Are they engaged, responsive, spontaneous?

- Use your intuition – watch for signs of discomfort, hesitation.

- Use goals and signposts or other objective measures of progress.

- Define stages of achievement so that you both know you are making progress.

- Do they come to you voluntarily?

How do I give good feedback?

Feedback is a vital part of the learning process. It enables learners to get quality information about their performance and progress, thus enabling them to adjust and improve.

- Focus on the behaviour not the person.

- Focus on observation rather than inference, intuition or guesses.

- Focus on description rather than judgement.

- Be specific rather than general.

- Balance negative with positive.

How do I motivate them?

Motivation is important, and it is equally important to recognise that people's level of motivation will vary at different times, and according to progress. Motivating them when things get tough is a very useful skill.

- Create some vision – how does the world look at the other end of the rainbow?

- Find out what makes them tick – what do they need?

- Encourage them.

- Give praise where it is due.

- Keep a positive frame of mind.

- Acknowledge and register progress when it happens.

How do I deal with a failing or unproductive relationship?

With the best will in the world, things do not always turn out as we want. It is important not just to press on regardless if you are not getting on.

- Diagnosis first – decisions later. Discuss these things openly.

- Check out what they think is happening, and how they feel.

- Reflect on and record your own misgivings.

- Try to identify and describe problems in a detailed and specific way rather than a generalised way.

- Use your support to discuss it.

- Check what provision there is or what procedures have been defined for mentors or learners who are unhappy.

- Make a plan for improvement or recovery, and then monitor it.

How do I do a training needs analysis?

An analysis of their own needs is a good discipline for anyone entering a development programme. It can help them to take stock, and to develop the agenda for their future development activities.

- Look at the requirements of their current job roles.

- Get them to define their future career aspirations and the associated requirements.

- Get them to make a statement of their strengths and weaknesses. Focus on skills, knowledge and competence.

- Get them to analyse their achievements and experiences at work.

- Get them to describe critical incidents to identify things they do well and those that they do less well.

199

How do I bring the relationship to an end?

Mentoring relationships should have a finite lifetime. Quite often, the duration of the relationship is specified at the outset. Even then, it needs to be managed properly.

- Is there a specified period for the duration of the relationship?

- Is the relationship tied to specific achievements or outcomes?

- Monitor progress and the lifecycle of the relationship.

- Define signposts or outcomes that will signify end points.

- Give notice and discuss it.

- You may need to re-define the relationship at various stages – for instance you may wish to continue seeing each other as friends, or on some other basis.

How do I ensure I am a high quality mentor?

Most professionals will want to be or work towards quality in all that they do. Like most work based activities, the plan-action-monitor-evaluate cycle is a good way to manage this.

- What do you mean by high quality mentor? Are there any objective ways of measuring success?

- What does your learner mean by high quality mentor?

- Prepare for sessions, and set goals and objectives.

- Work by consensus and agreement.

- Keep yourself up to date, and get development where necessary.

- Monitor progress – both your own and that of your learner. Mark achievements and celebrate success.

- Take stock every once in a while.

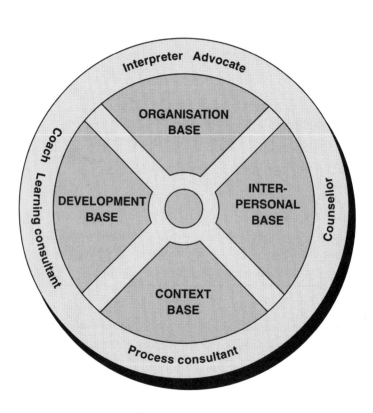

The 'One Stop' Mentor

■ ■ ■

■ Role models

The *organisation base* is associated with the roles of:

■ **Advocate or opportunity provider.** This is someone who can create opportunities for people to learn or to develop competence. The role is associated with the positional strength or the credibility within the organisation.

■ **Interpreter.** Here, the mentor offers managerial or organisational perspectives based on their wider knowledge of this or other organisations. They are also transmitters of the culture of the organisation by virtue of knowing the ropes.

The *context base* is associated with the role of:

■ **Process consultant.** In this role the mentor helps the learner to make sense of the broader requirements of the specific relationship (particularly if it is in a specific or structured learning programme). The mentor will be involved here with defining objectives, monitoring progress, solving problems, and so on.

The *development base* is associated with the roles of:

■ **Learning consultant.** This is someone who is able to act as a consultant adviser or resourcer on matters associated with learning.

■ **Coach.** Mentors quite often, by virtue of their wider and more senior experience or expertise, are able to coach their learners. That is, they can intervene directly to pass on knowledge and understanding, or to help them to develop skills.

The *interpersonal base* is associated with the role of:

■ **Counsellor.** A counsellor is someone who acts in the best interest of an individual. They have a high degree of empathy and communication skills. Here, we don't mean a counsellor necessarily in the therapeutic sense of the term. We use it in a much broader sense to include friend, adviser, guide, guardian, and so on.

Each of these roles can be described in terms of a particular set of *skills* and is related to the personal *qualities* that any mentor might bring to the role.

All of these roles and requirements come together in a set of *tasks and processes* that define the progress of the mentor – learner relationship. This whole array of interdependent factors is shown integrated into the mentoring wheel.

204

■ *Mentoring tasks*

1 Interpreter

When necessary, the interpreter helps the learner to understand the nature and the workings of the organisation. Interpreters can describe, explain and clarify:

- The organisation's mission and objectives
- Its structure, policies and procedures
- Its norms, values and management style
- How the organisation relates to the outside world
- How work is organised
- How the organisation relates to its markets and to its customers.

2 Advocate

205

Advocates know how to make things happen, get things done, and win understanding and support because they:

- Maintain informal and formal contacts with a wide range of the organisation's managers and opinion leaders
- Know how to operate effectively in the organisational culture and how to get things done
- Identify who should be involved in supporting the programme and seek their support
- Communicate the objectives and the benefits of the programme
- Represent the learner's interests to the senior management of the organisation.

3 Maintaining a relationship

Mentors establish and maintain a constructive and helpful relationship with the learner because they:

- Are readily accessible to the learner and, within reason, make time available when required

- Ask the right questions to make the learner think and come up with answers that matter

- Strike a good balance between giving direction and help and enabling the learner to set his/her own direction

- Act as a confidante to the learners

- Counsel the learners where appropriate.

4 Process consultant

Process consultants establish a mutual understanding with the learners of how they will manage the learning process to achieve objectives and how their relationship will support the learner because they:

- Help the learner to set a realistic time-frame for the achievement of the learning objectives and motivate the learner to keep to it

- Agree a clear framework of how often, when and where they will meet

- Give the learner honest and constructive feedback.

5 Learning consultant

Learning consultants identify and help the learners to find and use learning opportunities because they:

- Help to analyse strengths, weaknesses and needs

- Generate and examine a broad range of options and alternatives

- Suggest appropriate assignments or projects in which suitable learning can take place

- Use appropriate questioning to maximise learning from experience

- Help the learner to set learning goals

- Coach where appropriate.

■ *Mentor qualities*

1. **Management perspective.** Someone who has experience of, and competence in, management. Alternatively, through experience working with managers in organisations, someone who has had widespread exposure to and understands management practice and pressures.

2. **Organisational know-how.** Someone who knows how to get things done within the organisational system in which the learner works.

3. **Credibility.** Someone who enjoys personal and professional credibility, either in his/her own right or with the members of the organisation in which the learner works.

4. **Accessibility.** Someone who is able to make him/herself available to others when they need it.

5. **Communication.** Someone who has a strong range of interpersonal skills and can tune in to others' ideas, views and feelings.

6. **Empowering orientation.** Someone who creates a climate and the conditions in which it is safe for individuals to try out different ways of doing things, to contribute more fully, and to have a greater share in what is going on in their organisation.

7. **Developmental orientation.** Someone who has experience of and takes a keen and active interest in others' development.

8. **Inventiveness.** Someone who is open to new ideas and to different ways of doing things; someone who perceives different and useful connections and patterns, and is a good, creative problem-solver in his/her own right.

(This list was developed by Dr Brian O'Neill.)

207

■ *Implementation checklist*

1 Is the organisation ready and capable?

2 Have aims and goals been defined?

3 Is there commitment from the top, and is this visible?

4 Has a champion or project manager been appointed?

5 Are there criteria for selecting mentors?

6 Are there criteria for selecting learners?

7 Are the mentors to be trained?

8 Is there a system for matching mentors and learners?

9 Have terms of reference been set and guidelines given?

10 Are there systems for monitoring and evaluating in place?

11 Are there contingency plans to deal with problems?

Index

■ ■ ■

accessibility 39, 40, 43, 160
 importance of 46, 47
 and terms of reference 140–1
activists 104
added value 4
adult education 97, 98
advocates 30–1, 67, 69–71, 144
affirmative action 79–80
agendas 142–3, 194
 social agenda 122–3
AMI Healthcare 79
attributes of mentors 38–47

Barham, Kevin 81
behaviour of mentors 72
benefits from mentoring 9–11
 for learners 11–13, 22
 for mentors 13–14
 for organisations 15
 value-added 160–1
body language 124–5
Brent Council 79
British Alcan 78
British Gas 78–9

Cannon and Taylor Working Party
 5, 13
career enhancement 12, 14, 85
Carter, Steve 25
champions 178–9
change 3–9, 64
 and learners 165–7
 in learning 7–9
 and management 5–7, 66–7
 in organisations 4, 65–7
chemistry 168
choosing mentors 47–51, 84, 157,
 180–2
Clutterbuck, David 9–10
coaching 31, 33, 109–16, 195–6
communication 39, 40–1, 43, 46,

47, 120, 159
 non-verbal 124–6
 in organisations 66
 tripartite model 71
Competent Manager Programme
 23–6, 70, 86
competition 4
conceptualisation 101, 103
conduct of relationships 144
confidence curves 98–9, 150
confidentiality 52, 140
conflict in relationships 49, 50–1,
 168–9, 198–9
consumers 3–4
context base 28, 78–92
 and induction of graduates 45
 points of focus 86–8
 role models 31, 203
Conway, Christopher 81
corporate schemes 59–62
counselling 31, 33, 58, 127–33,
 195–6
credibility 39, 40, 42–3, 69
 importance of 46, 47
cross-functional relationships 175,
 176
cultural diversity 79–80
culture 12, 15, 27–8, 63–6, 186
customers 3–4

Derby mentoring project 80
development base 28–9, 96–116
 and induction of graduates 45
 points of focus 88
 role models 31, 203
developmental orientation 39, 41,
 44, 116
 importance of 46, 47
dimensions of relationships 82–4

economy 3

employee benefits from mentoring 11–13
employment 5
empowering orientation 39, 41, 44, 116
  importance of 46, 47
empowerment 4, 6, 13, 15, 32
endorsement of programmes 175
ethnic minorities in management 178
ethos 121, 139
evaluation of programmes 182–5
experience 101, 102
experimentation 101, 103–4
external mentors 62, 176

feedback 10–11, 13, 112–13, 126–7, 151, 197–8
first session 193
formal mentors 157
formal relationships 83
four-base model of relationships 26–9
functional base 27–8

goals 72, 91, 142, 160
group discussion 185

hi-key programmes 184
Honey, D. 104

induction 45–6, 165
informal relationships 83
innovation 66
Institute of Management 23–6, 70, 86
internal mentors 62, 176
international managers 81
interpersonal base 29, 120–34
  and induction of graduates 46
  points of focus 88–9
  roles models 31, 203–4
interpersonal skills 159
interpreters 31, 67, 68, 144
interviews 184
inventiveness 39, 41, 44–5, 46, 47

jo-hari window 131

Kolb learning cycle 100–3

learners
  benefits of mentoring 11–13, 22
  and change 166–7
  and choice of mentors 49–50
  confidence curve 98–9, 150
  contributions from 169
  expectations of 159–62
  fears of 162–4
  preparing for mentoring 164–5
  setting objectives 91
learning 96–7, 195
  adult education 97, 98
  changes in 7–9
  consultants 31, 109, 144
  contract 141
  Kolb learning cycle 100–3
  styles 104–8, 106–8, 149
Library and Information Service (LIS) 78
life-cycle 138–52
  growth and performance 143–51
  initiation 139–43
  maturity 151–2
line managers
  as mentors 51–2, 60
  support of 192–3
listening 127
lo-key programmes 184–5
logos 123

McLean, Norman 80
management
  and change 5–7, 66–7
  mentors' experience of 39–40, 42, 46, 47, 69
  project management 72
  time management 72, 91, 140–1
managers
  benefits from mentoring 13–14
  as coaches 114
  coping with change 5–7
  as developers of people 97–8
  development of 8
  international 81
  line managers 51–2, 60, 192–3
  project-manager champions 178, 179

women 178, 182–3
markets 3–4
mentoring definition 20, 23
mentoring wheel 30–3
mind mapping 113–14
monitoring programmes 182–5
monitoring progress 92
moral dimension of relationships
    121
motivation 161–2, 166–7, 198
Mumford, A. 104

National Mentoring Consortium
    80–1
natural mentoring 20–2, 83–4, 157
negative mentoring 58
non-verbal communication 124–6
NVQs (National Vocational Qualifi-
    cations) 23, 25, 52, 86

objectives 91, 142, 160
    organisational objectives 63
    SMART objectives 91, 111, 112
Occupational Standards for Man-
    agement 23–5
one-to-one relationships 123–7
O'Neill, Dr Brian 39
open-framed relationships 83–4
opportunity providers 30–1
organisation base 27–8, 58–74
    and induction graduates 45
    points of focus 85–6
    roles models 30–1, 203
organisational culture 12, 15, 27–8,
    63–6, 186
organisational know-how 39, 40, 42,
    46, 47, 69
organisational objectives 63
organisational structure 65–6
organisations
    benefits from mentoring 15
    and change 4, 65–7
    communications 66
    corporate schemes 59–62
    and mentoring relationships 192

pathos 121–3, 139
performance 13, 110
personal relationships 12, 21–2

personal satisfaction 14
planning programmes 178–80, 185
political control 185–6
positional strength 72–4
pragmatists 106
preparation for mentoring role
    190–2
problem-solving 13, 41, 132, 145–9
process consultants 31, 87, 90–3,
    144
programmes 175–86
    aims 177–8
    endorsement 175
    hi-key 184
    lo-key 184–5
    management infrastructure 174
    monitoring 182–5
    planning 178–80, 185
    problems in 185–6
    resourcing 174, 178–80
    selecting mentors 47–51, 84, 157,
        180–2
    training mentors 52–3, 87,
        180–2, 199
progress monitoring 92–3
project management 72
project-manager champions 178,
    179

qualities of mentors 38–47, 151,
    156
questionnaires 183

rapport 126, 139
reflection 101, 103
reflectors 105
relationships
    changes in 5
    components 120–3
    conduct 144
    conflict 49, 50–1, 168–9, 198–9
    and corporate schemes 59–62
    cross-functional 175, 176
    dimensions 82–4
    ending 199–200
    formal 83
    four-base model 26–9
    informal 83
    and learning styles 106–8

letting go 133–4, 199–200
moral dimension 121
one-to-one 123–7
open-framed 83–4
personal 12, 21–2
structured 83–4
terms of reference 32–3, 181
at work 23–7
see also life-cycle
resourcing 174, 178–80
respect 159
role conflict 168, 176
role enhancement 14
role models 30–3, 67, 71–4, 109–10, 160, 203–4
role-model champions 178–9
roles
of managers 7
of mentors 2–3, 28, 191–2

schools 78
selecting mentors 47–51, 84, 157, 180–2
self-awareness 131
self-development 8–9, 14
skills 12, 14, 31
lack of 168
of mentors 38–47
SMART objectives 91, 111, 112
social agenda 122–3
staff benefits from mentoring 11–13

structured relationships 83–4
style
of learning 104–8, 106–8, 149
of mentoring 149–51, 160, 168, 194–5
supporting mentors 196

tasks of mentoring 144–5
teams 4, 7, 13
technological development 3, 4
terms of reference 32–3, 139–41, 181
theorising 101, 103
theorists 105–6
3D approach to coaching 111–14
3D approach to counselling 129–32
time management 72, 91, 140–1
training mentors 52–3, 87, 180–2, 199
tripartite model of communication 71
TSB 79

value-added benefits 160–1
voice tone 125–6
women in management 178, 182–3
words 124
work relationships 23–7
workplace changes 4